大学英语自主听力进阶之一

# LISTENING FOR SUCCESS
# INTERVIEWS

主编 王敏华 陈希茹
编者 王敏华 沈 璟 邵 蕙 陈希茹

访谈篇

上海外语教育出版社
外教社 SHANGHAI FOREIGN LANGUAGE EDUCATION PRESS

图书在版编目（CIP）数据

大学英语自主听力进阶. 你问我答访谈篇 / 王敏华，陈希茹主编.
一上海：上海外语教育出版社，2009（2016重印）
ISBN 978-7-5446-0591-5

Ⅰ. 大… Ⅱ. ①王…②陈… Ⅲ. 英语－听说教学－高等学校－教材
Ⅳ. H319.9

中国版本图书馆CIP数据核字（2007）第157894号

出版发行：上海外语教育出版社
（上海外国语大学内） 邮编：200083
电　　话：021-65425300（总机）
电子邮箱：bookinfo@sflep.com.cn
网　　址：http://www.sflep.com.cn http://www.sflep.com
责任编辑：杭　海

印　　刷：上海华业装璜印刷厂有限公司
开　　本：787×1092 1/16 印张 14 字数 370 千字
版　　次：2009 年 5月第 1版 2016 年 7月第 9次印刷
印　　数：1 500 册

书　　号：ISBN 978-7-5446-0591-5 / G・0286
定　　价：29.00 元

# 编者的话

## 关于“大学英语自主听力进阶”系列

听力理解的成功基于听者的语言知识和背景知识的相互作用。语言知识主要包括语音、词汇和句法知识等，背景知识则包括对讲话人的熟识程度、对所讲话题的熟识程度等。但有实验表明，英语学习者在听英语时主要依赖语言知识进行理解，也就是说他们的注意力集中在通过语音表达的词汇和句法结构上。这是因为听英语不同于听我们的母语，听者无暇顾及语言以外的东西。

“大学英语自主听力进阶”系列即针对这一现象专门编写，希望英语学习者在听英语时不仅关注词汇和句法结构，还要关注听力材料的背景知识和篇章结构，这样有助于更好地理解所听内容。关注篇章结构从某种意义上来说就等于注意到了句子间的联系，因而也会提高听者对所听内容的记忆强度。

“大学英语自主听力进阶”系列共分四册：《你问我答访谈篇》、《轻松睿智故事篇》、《东西南北新闻篇》和《智慧之桥讲座篇》。每册分别含有二十个单元，每个单元由Before You Listen，Listen Now，Look at This 和 Here's More 四个部分组成。各部分的主要内容和功能如下：

- Before You Listen 相当于听前热身。这部分由提问和预测 Listen Now 部分课文大意两个项目组成。在回答 Before You Listen 部分提出的问题时，听者可以激活和本单元听力内容相关的背景知识，然后浏览整个单元提供的信息（包括词汇），对 Listen Now 的大意进行预测。
- Listen Now 由两篇听力课文组成。每篇课文配有：1）词汇注释；2）对 Before You Listen 部分课文大意预测的核实练习；3）两到三项针对课文的练习。
- Look at This 针对 Listen Now 部分的听力内容提出需要注意的问题，作专门讲解。这些问题有的和读音或词句相关，有的和篇章相关，还有的则和听力内容的背景知识相关。
- Here's More 针对 Look at This 提供听力实践的机会。

以上四个部分一环扣一环，使每个单元成为一个有机的整体。而四本分册涉及日常听力活动中常见的四种体裁，难度依次递升，也使整个系列成为一个有机的整体。归纳起来，本系列图书有以下四个特点：

1、选材真实，原汁原味，既学语言，又学文化；

2、遵循认知规律，注重听前激活、听时兴趣、听后反思；

3、针对英语学习者听力理解中的普遍难点（如连词和生词等引起的听力障碍）进行精要讲解，并提供专项训练，帮助听者积累和掌握听力技能，充分体验学习和成功的喜悦；

4、听力理解与相关背景知识的掌握息息相关，因此本系列图书有针对性地介绍了和听力材料相关的背景知识。背景知识积累得越多，越有利于听力理解。

本系列的每本分册建议按如下步骤使用：

1、尝试回答每单元第一部分 Think and answer 中的提问，以激活头脑中和本单元内容有关的背景知识；

2、浏览本单元提供的信息，如词汇、练习题等，对听力材料的主要内容进行预测，以便积极主动地投入到听力实践中去；

3、听 Text One 以核实或调整预测；

4、听第二遍或第三遍，做 Text One 中其余的练习；

5、听 Text Two 以核实或调整预测；

6、听第二遍或第三遍，做 Text Two 中其余的练习；

7、阅读 Look at This；

8、做 Here's More 提供的练习。

希望英语学习者在使用"大学英语自主听力进阶"系列图书的过程中，能够感受到同一体裁听力材料的共性，从而积极主动地获取信息，这将有助于听力理解和听力记忆。我们相信，如果英语学习者能认真听完每一本分册，一定会受益匪浅，顺利通过英语专业或非专业的各类听力考试应该是意料之中的事。

## 关于本系列第一册《你问我答访谈篇》

访谈的总体框架是问答。采访人起话题导向作用，在被采访人就某一话题展开阐述时，采访人通过评论、归纳、总结、发问等使谈话进行下去。一般也是由采访人通过上述方式引领谈话从一个话题转到另一个话题。因此我们可以说采访人引出话题，而被采访人提供细节。当然有时也会有例外。本分册中的访谈材料可以使您对这一交流形式有更多深入的了解。

## 致谢

本分册第一至十单元 Text One 和 Text Two 的内容为编者之一在美国 St. Olaf College 进修期间所作的采访，采访对象大多为该校的任课教授，整个过程还得到了校方的大力支持，在此我们对参加采访的各位教授和 St. Olaf College 表示由衷的感谢。本分册第十八至二十单元的内容为华东师范大学英语教学部赵国霞老师对美籍教师Curtis Evans的采访，在此我们也对他们两位表示由衷的感谢。

编者

2009 年 1 月

# Contents

# Unit 1

# Clothes

## Part One Before You Listen

### I. Think and answer

1. What do you usually wear when you go to school or work?
2. What do you wear when you visit your friends or relatives?
3. Do you wear casual clothes or a suit when you travel for pleasure?
4. What colors are in fashion this year?
5. Do you buy or make your clothes? Why?

### II. Make your prediction

*Browse through all the information offered in this unit and predict the main idea of Text One and Text Two by choosing from a, b, c and d. You may choose more than one answer to indicate your prediction.*

**Text One**

a. The latest fashion.
b. Clothes people wear at work.
c. Fashion industry.
d. Clothes people wear on different occasions.

**Text Two**

a. Clothes and social status.
b. Sources of people's clothes.

c. Colors and clothes in fashion.
d. Styles of clothes.

## Part Two Listen Now

### Text One

#### I. Words and expressions

slacks /slæks/ *n.* 宽松的长裤
tuxedo /tʌkˈsiːdəʊ/ *n.* 男子礼服
sequin /ˈsiːkwɪn/ *n.* 闪光装饰片
bead /biːd/ *n.* 珠子
midriff /ˈmɪdrɪf/ *n.* 上腹部
corsage /kɔːˈsɑːʒ/ *n.* 装饰花束
fancy /ˈfænsɪ/ *adj.* 花哨的；别致的

#### II. Listen to confirm or to adjust

*Listen and find out if your expectations are the same as or different from what you hear. If different, find the correct one or ones from **Make your prediction**.*

#### III. Listen and choose the best answer to each question you hear.

1. a. Shirts.
   b. Special dresses.
   c. Tuxedoes.
   d. Sweaters.

2. a. Fancy clothes.
   b. Comfortable clothes.
   c. Special clothes.
   d. Cheap clothes.

3. a. A tuxedo.
   b. A long dress.
   c. Jewelry.
   d. A corsage.

## IV. Listen and complete the following table with the missing information.

| Occasions | | Clothes to wear | |
|---|---|---|---|
| formal | going to church | 1. ______ | |
| | 2. ______ | long dresses | 3. ______ |
| | 4. dances &______ | 5. ______ | |
| informal | 6. ______ | 8. ______ | 9. ______ |
| | 7. ______ | 10. ______ | 11. ______ |
| | shopping | 12. ______ | 13. ______ |

# Text Two

## I. Words and expressions

formality /fɔːˈmæləti/ *n.* 正式；礼节
subsidiary /səbˈsɪdɪəri/ *n.* 子公司
economical /ˌiːkəˈnɒmɪkəl/ *adj.* 节俭的，精打细算的
beige /beɪʒ/ *adj.* 米黄色的
navy /ˈneɪvi/ *adj.* 深蓝色的
pinpoint /ˈpɪnpɔɪnt/ *v.* 准确地描述
flower girl 女花童（在婚礼行列中执花或撒花的女孩）
Oregon /ˈɒrɪgən/ 俄勒冈州（美国）
Portland /ˈpɔːtlənd/ 波特兰（美国俄勒冈州西北部港市）

## II. Listen to confirm or to adjust

*Listen and find out if your expectations are the same as or different from what you hear. If different, find the correct one or ones from* ***Make your prediction****.*

## III. Listen and answer the following questions.

1. What affects the choices of clothes people wear at work?

_______________________________________________

2. Why does Barbara prefer to make her own clothes?

_______________________________________________

3. What are the colors for next year?

_______________________________________________

## IV. Listen and fill in the following blanks with the missing information.

1. To some extent, the clothes people wear disclose their ________________.
2. In a subsidiary office, Barbara's son prefers to wear ____________________ instead of a ____________.
3. Barbara now buys ____________________ than before.
4. People prefer to wear what makes them ____________________ and therefore it's difficult for Barbara to pinpoint any ________________________.

# Part Three Look at This

### 去除赘述，获取实质性的信息

在口语中，特别是即兴讲话时，讲话人经常会犹豫、重复或中途改变主意，甚至所讲的话不符合语法规则。请看下列句子：

1. … like going to church, you might, people might, women might have a special dress that they wear …
2. … sometimes they wear jeans, aah … aah knit shirts …
3. … where people usually, women usually wear slacks …

因而在听的过程中，听话人应该学会去除赘述以获取实质性的信息。方法如下：

1. 从上下文判断讲话人真正要表述的意思;
2. 特别注意讲话人改口的部分;
3. 特别注意类似 I mean，no 这样的词组或词。在这样的词组或词后面通常是讲话人要更正或详细说明的内容。

## Part Four Here's More

### Exercise

*You will hear a number of sentences. Listen and write down the main messages that the speaker intends to convey.*

**Example:**

You hear: I wonder … I mean I was wondering … if you might possibly … if you would like to go to the show with me? I mean the fashion show.

The main message: Would you like to go to the fashion show with me?

Now it's your turn to write down the main messages of the sentences you hear.

1. ______________________________
2. ______________________________
3. ______________________________
4. ______________________________
5. ______________________________
6. ______________________________
7. ______________________________
8. ______________________________
9. ______________________________
10. ______________________________
11. ______________________________
12. ______________________________
13. ______________________________
14. ______________________________
15. ______________________________

# Unit 2

# Food

## Part One Before You Listen

### I. Think and answer

1. Do you sometimes cook?
2. Can you describe the process in which a dish is cooked?
3. What do you usually have for breakfast, lunch and supper?
4. Do you sometimes entertain guests at home?
5. What do you entertain the guests with?
6. Are there any specific rules for you to lay the table when you entertain guests at home?

### II. Make your prediction

*Browse through all the information offered in this unit and predict the main idea of Text One and Text Two by choosing from a, b, c and d. You may choose more than one answer to indicate your prediction.*

**Text One**

a. Making a pie and cooking meals.
b. Eating meals.
c. Having a party.
d. Entertaining guests.

**Text Two**

a. Cooking utensils.
b. Three meals and entertaining guests.
c. Family reunion.
d. Something to drink.

## Part Two Listen Now

### Text One

#### I. Words and expressions

pumpkin /ˈpʌmpkɪn/ *n.* 南瓜
challenge /ˈtʃælɪndʒ/ *n.*，*v.* 挑战
crust /krʌst/ *n.* 点心的油酥皮
shortening /ˈʃɔːtənɪŋ/ *n.* 油酥（拌在面粉里使糕点松脆的油脂）
pastry /ˈpeɪstrɪ/ *n.* （面粉加油脂、牛奶或水揉成的）油酥面团
blender /ˈblendə/ *n.* （厨房用电动）食品搅拌器
flaky /ˈfleɪkɪ/ *adj.* 易碎成片的；酥的
tender /ˈtendə/ *adj.* 嫩的；软的
spice /spaɪs/ *n.* 香料，调味品
cinnamon /ˈsɪnəmən/ *n.* 桂皮香料
nutmeg /ˈnʌtmeg/ *n.* 肉豆蔻
custard /ˈkʌstəd/ *n.* 乳蛋糕
extensive /ɪkˈstensɪv/ *adj.* 大量的；广泛的
custard pie 蛋奶馅饼
push into 揉挤（面团）
roll out （把面团）擀开

#### II. Listen to confirm or to adjust

*Listen and find out if your expectations are the same as or different from what you hear. If different, find the correct one or ones from **Make your prediction**.*

#### III. Listen and give a short answer to each of the following questions and fill in the blanks where necessary with the missing information.

1. What pie did Barbara make?

______________________________

2. A crust is made of pastry and is essential in making a pumpkin pie. Following are the procedures to make this pie. Some of the words are left out and please fill in the blanks with the missing words.

   a. Mix flour, __________, salt and water.
   b. Use a pastry __________ to cut the ___________ into the flour.
   c. _________ the pastry into and roll it out.
   d. Put the pastry in a pie _________.
   e. Mix pumpkin, ________, milk and _________ to make a custard.
   f. Put the custard on ________ of the crust in the ________.
   g. __________ the pie for about __________ at a low _________________.

3. Who is now living with Barbara?

   ______________________________________________________________________

4. What type of meals does Barbara prepare?

   ______________________________________________________________________

5. How many hours does Barbara spend when she cooks something extensive?

   ______________________________________________________________________

## IV. Listen and decide whether the following statements are true (T) or false (F).

1. Pumpkin pie is a kind of dessert people in USA serve on Thanksgiving Day. T ☐ F ☐
2. Pumpkin pie is very easy to make. T ☐ F ☐
3. Barbara's family is childless. T ☐ F ☐
4. Barbara used to cook a lot of things for one meal. T ☐ F ☐
5. Barbara is not good at cooking so she often cooks something simple. T ☐ F ☐

# Text Two

## I. Words and expressions

cereal /ˈsɪərɪəl/ *n.* 谷类食品(如玉米片等)
toast /təʊst/ *n.* 吐司(烤面包片)

pancake /ˈpænkeɪk/ *n.* 薄煎饼
stir-fry /ˈstɜːfraɪ/ *v.* 爆炒
nutritious /njuːˈtrɪʃəs/ *adj.* 有营养的
entertain /ˌentəˈteɪn/ *v.* 款待
grill /grɪl/ *n.* 烤架
casserole /ˈkæsərəʊl/ *n.* 炖锅，砂锅；砂锅菜
roast /rəʊst/ *n.* 大块烤肉
utensil /juːˈtensəl/ *n.* 器皿；用具
napkin /ˈnæpkɪn/ *n.* 餐巾
scrambled eggs 炒蛋
fried eggs 煎蛋
on an informal basis 非正式地

## II. Listen to confirm or to adjust

*Listen and find out if your expectations are the same as or different from what you hear. If different, find the correct one or ones from **Make your prediction**.*

## III. Listen and pick up words from the box to complete the following two tables.

| | | | |
|---|---|---|---|
| casserole | cereal | coffee | dessert |
| fried eggs | juice | meat | milk |
| pancakes | roast | salad | sandwiches |
| scrambled eggs | soups | stir-fry dish | toast with jam |
| vegetables | | | |

| Meals | Food |
|---|---|
| Breakfast | 1. ________ |
| Lunch | 2. ________ |
| Supper | 3. ________ |

| | Entertaining Guests at Home |
|---|---|
| First served | 4. ________ |
| Main dish | 5. ________ |
| Last served | 6. ________ |

## IV. Listen and answer the following questions.

1. Which meal is considered the most nutritious and most relaxing?
______________________________
2. What is regarded as informal when guests are entertained?
______________________________
3. At a formal dinner, where do guests sit?
______________________________
4. Where is the fork placed?
______________________________
5. How and where is the knife put?
______________________________
6. Where is the spoon?
______________________________
7. Where is the water glass?
______________________________

# Part Three Look at This

### 叙述做事步骤

在Text One的采访中，Barbara叙述了做pumpkin pie的过程。她在讲述时用了一系列动词，如mix together，cut … into …，push ... into，roll ... out，put，pour … into … 等，动作的先后按这些动词出现的先后而定。这中间她用了一个表示顺序的词，即then。

在描述做一件事的过程时，大致就这样：一系列表示不同动作的动词，先做的先说，后做的后说，间或插一两个表示顺序的信号词，如first，second，then等，或者用before，after，until等连词引出时间状语从句以表示动作的先后。

因而我们在听这类材料时，应注意以下事项：

1. 关注表示动作的动词；
2. 关注表示顺序的信号词；
3. 关注表示动作先后的时间状语从句。

# Part Four Here's More

In this part you will hear four passages that describe the procedures for doing things.

## Exercise One

*Listen to the two passages and rearrange the order of the following phrases.*

**Passage One Is Your Bathtub Discolored?**

a. Remove the soaked towels.

b. Soak paper towels in full strength vinegar.

c. Cover the tub in paper towels.

**Passage Two Clean Blankets with a Professional Look**

a. Add the detergent.

b. Set the cycle.

c. Wash on gentle.

d. Add the blanket.

e. Add 1-1/2 cups of white vinegar in the final rinse.

## Exercise Two

*Listen to the two passages and fill in the following blanks with the missing information.*

**Passage One Try This Recipe for Some "Play Clay"**

a. __________ 2-1/2 cups of ________ and 1 cup of water until just __________.

b. Then _________ 1-1/2 cups of cornstarch with 3/4 cup of water.

c. ________ this to the salt and water __________.

d. ________ until it is _________.

e. If necessary, _________ more water or cornstarch for consistency.

f. _________ until it is ________.

g. _________ and __________ it in the refrigerator.

**Passage Two How to Remove Candle Wax from the Carpet**

a. ___________ off as much wax as you can, using a _________ knife.

b. Then __________ the spot with ___________ toweling and _____________ the spot (synthetic setting).

c. The napkin will show through wax. ___________ and __________ until all the wax is _________ from the carpet.

# Unit 3

# Real Estate

## Part One Before You Listen

### I. Think and answer

1. What is your house/apartment like?
2. Do you want to be a real estate agent?
3. Is it difficult to become a real estate agent?
4. What exactly does a real estate agent do?
5. How expensive is it to buy an apartment or a house in your area?
6. Do people in your country buy their properties on a mortgage?

### II. Make your prediction

*Browse through all the information offered in this unit and predict the main idea of Text One and Text Two by choosing from a, b, c and d. You may choose more than one answer to indicate your prediction.*

**Text One**

a. The process in which a real estate agent helps people sell their houses.
b. The qualification a real estate agent needs.
c. A computer course for real estate agents.
d. A successful real estate agent.

**Text Two**

a. Average prices of properties.

b. Expensive houses.
c. The percentage of people who can afford a house.
d. A mortgage program by the government.

# Part Two Listen Now

## Text One

### I. Words and expressions

property /ˈprɒpətɪ/ *n.* 房产，地产（和 real estate 意思相同）
realtor /ˈrɪəltə/ *n.*（美）房地产经纪人（和 real estate agent 意思相同）
mortgage /ˈmɔːɡɪdʒ/ *n.* 抵押贷款
broker /ˈbrəʊkə/ *n.* 经纪人，代理人
brokerage /ˈbrəʊkərɪdʒ/ *n.* 经纪业；佣金
stuff /stʌf/ *n.* 东西
landscaping /ˈlændˌskeɪpɪŋ/ *v.* 景观美化

### II. Listen to confirm or to adjust

*Listen and find out if your expectations are the same as or different from what you hear. If different, find the correct one or ones from* ***Make your prediction****.*

### III. Listen and decide whether the following statements are true (T) or false (F).

1. Mrs. Johnson has been a real estate agent for more than 20 years. T □ F □
2. In America, a realtor can easily keep his/her license as long as he/she pays license fees and dues to several associations every year. T □ F □

3. A realtor's salary depends on how many houses he/she markets within a month. *T* ☐ *F* ☐
4. A successful realtor is unwilling to spend extra money on high tech in his/her business because that is unnecessary. *T* ☐ *F* ☐
5. According to Mrs. Johnson, it is buyers that actually decide on the selling price of a house. *T* ☐ *F* ☐
6. Whether a house is sold out successfully or not, to some extent, depends on its image in the eyes of potential buyers. *T* ☐ *F* ☐

## IV. Listen and answer the following questions.

1. Why were houses in 1981 less affordable in America?

_______________________________________________

2. How many hours' further education must a realtor in America take each year?

_______________________________________________

3. When does a realtor find "Know your neighborhood" helpful?

_______________________________________________

4. What should be taken into account when a seller prices his/her house?

_______________________________________________

5. What does Mrs. Johnson suggest a house seller do if he/she has too much stuff?

_______________________________________________

# Text Two

## I. Words and expressions

medium /ˈmiːdɪəm/ *adj.* 中间的；适中的
condo /ˈkɒndəʊ/ *n.* 分套出售的公寓；个人购置的一套房间
quality /ˈkwɒlətɪ/ *n.* 质量；优质
rundown /ˈrʌnˈdaʊn/ *adj.* 情况不好的，状况糟糕的
back /bæk/ *v.* 援助，赞助
default /dɪˈfɔːlt/ *v., n.* 不履行；违约；拖欠
square foot 平方英尺
Arizona /ˌærɪˈzəʊnə/ 亚利桑那州（美国）

## II. Listen to confirm or to adjust

*Listen and find out if your expectations are the same as or different from what you hear. If different, find the correct one or ones from* ***Make your prediction****.*

## III. Listen and choose the right answer to complete each of the following sentences.

1. Mrs. Johnson gets statistics for the average price ________.
   a. from her computer
   b. from her colleagues
   c. from her buyers
   d. from her sellers

2. ________ is the closest in meaning to a "rambler."
   a. A mobile house
   b. A single-storey house
   c. A condo house
   d. A hobby farm

3. ________ of the people cannot afford to buy a house in Mrs. Johnson's area.
   a. 90%
   b. 90 to 95%
   c. 5 to 10%
   d. 10%

4. Mrs. Johnson is ________ about the government-assisted housing policy.
   a. suspicious
   b. optimistic
   c. pessimistic
   d. critical

5. ________ can benefit from the FHA (Federal Housing Authority) Chain Mortgage Program.
   a. Those who can't afford to buy a house
   b. Those who want to buy a second house
   c. Those who are in desperate need of a house
   d. Those who want to buy a house in Mrs. Johnson's area

## IV. Listen and fill in the following blanks with the missing information.

1. Mrs. Johnson provides more than one average price in her area because ________________.
2. A house built in 1994 with an area of _________ square feet may sell for US$ ________.

Its price may go up when ______________.

3. According to Mrs. Johnson, a condo house in her small town, on average, will sell for US$ ________ while a hobby farm for US$ ________.
4. The house for investment is ______________ among all the houses mentioned by Mrs. Johnson. On average, it sells for US$ ________. This can also explain why ____________ is the longest.
5. Generally, a mobile house is below US$ _______. One of Mrs. Johnson's realtor friends bought one at US$ __________. Surely, this price doesn't include the fees to ____________ ________________________________.
6. According to the interview, the FHA (Federal Housing Authority) Chain Mortgage Program covers the following aspects: _______________, ____________ and ____________.

## Part Three Look at This

### 多听多练，培养对数字的敏感度

我们在听有关数字的信息时往往会感到困难，例如，在听一些较大的数字或分辨“十几”和“几十”的时候，会一下子感到没有头绪。请看以下句子中的数字：

1. I mean 40,000, you can get a brand new one.
2. So uh ... that would leave you with the mortgage of 113,760 ...
3. ... so for that purchase of 115,200, the, with the 3% down, and that would be a principle on interest to 790 dollars ...

在听 40,000 时可能一下子反应不过来，这是因为在汉语里是用“万”来表示“几十千”的；而在听 113,760 时，容易误听成 130,760，这是因为 113 和 130 听上去有点相似。

在我们听过的这篇采访中数字用来表示房价，当然，用数字表达的不仅仅有价格，还有时间、日期、电话号码及各类编号，如邮政编码、座位号、门牌号、银行账号、飞机航班号等。数字如此频繁地出现在日常生活中，所以在听英语时免不了要过数字关。在听、说数字时，需要注意的地方很多，完全掌握它们需要一点一滴地进行听力实践，慢慢积累，不断总结，以达到轻松自如地听懂并记住数字的境界。

以下罗列的建议虽不能面面俱到，但值得大家注意:

1. 平时就培养对数字的敏感度。

比如，随意写下一些数字，用英语读出。也可以和同学合作做游戏，每人写下一组数字，看谁可以在最短时间内用英语正确读出对方给出的数字。

2. 注意数字的读音。

表示“十几”的数字重音在后，如thir'teen；而表示“几十”的数字重读在前，如'thirty；并且前者结尾元音是长音 /iː/，后者是短音 /ɪ/。

3. 注意英语中的数字表达，从右到左以三位数为一单元。

（注：口语中可省略不读 hundred 后面的 and，比如 186 也可读作 one hundred eighty-six。）

4. 了解不同的数字表达方式和读法。

例如：(1) 小数和分数的读法。比如：小数 0.23 可以读作 zero (或 nought) point two three (或 twenty-three)，也可读成 point two three (或 twenty-three)；分数 1/4 可以读作 one fourth 或 a/one quarter。(2) 在表达两个或三个相同的数字时可以用 double 或 triple 来代替。比如：67803533 中的 33 可以读作 three three 或 double three; Lane 555 中的 555 可以读作 five five five 或 triple five。

5. 了解英语国家的人们在表达数字时的一些习惯。

例如：(1) 电话号码。7 位数字的号码读的时候前三位一组、后四位一组连在一起，中间有一个停顿，比如 3254898 读作 three two five (pause) four eight nine eight; 8 位数字的号码可以四个一组来读。(2) 价格。在口语中，说价格时货币单位可以省略不读，如 $14.50 可以读作 fourteen dollars fifty cents，也可直接读作 fourteen fifty。

6. 某些情况下，数字和字母连用。

例如：在表示（英国还有其他一些国家的）邮政编码、飞机或火车上的座位号等等时，数字和字母可连用。

## Part Four Here's More

### Exercise One

*Listen to the statements and fill in the blanks with the numbers you hear.*

1. Your flight number is ________ and you have a seat numbered ______, next to the window.
2. The foods cost $______.
3. It is wet and cool in Scotland or Northern Ireland this weekend and the temperatures will fall to ______ °F.
4. Don't forget the appointment at _______ tomorrow.
5. _____ of the people surveyed gave journalists high ethical ratings in 1981.
6. The World Trade Center had a big office space — _______________m² — for 500 large companies.

7. Our turnover soared to £______________ last year.
8. The population in my country is ____________________.

## Exercise Two

*Listen to the conversations and complete the following tables.*

**Conversation One: Ordering Items from a Library**

**City Central Library**

**Request Form**

Name: Lester Mackie

Membership No. (1) ___________

Address: (2) _____ Westmead Road, Annandale

Phone No.: (3) _________ for day time

(4) _________ after 5 p.m.

Fax No.: (5) ___________

**Conversation Two: Applying for the Telephone Banking Service**

**Application Form for Banking Services**

*Customer's information:*

Name: John Peter Barnard

Address: 24 Manor Road Winchester

Postcode: (6) _________

Date of birth: Oct (7) _________

Phone number: (8) _________

*Account details:*

Sort code: (9) ___________

Account number: (10) __________

# Unit 4

# Transportation and Traveling

## Part One Before You Listen

### I. Think and answer

1. How do you go to work or study every day? By car, bus, subway, rapid transit, taxi or bicycle?
2. How much time do you spend on your way?
3. What do you do on your way?
4. Do you travel during your holiday?
5. Where do you usually go on holiday and how do you go?

### II. Make your prediction

*Browse through all the information offered in this unit and predict the main idea of Text One and Text Two by choosing from a, b, c and d. You may choose more than one answer to indicate your prediction.*

**Text One**

a. How people in different places go to work.
b. How people in Northfield go to work.
c. Transportation in Minneapolis.
d. Transportation in New York.

### Text Two

a. Why people prefer to travel by car.
b. Why people prefer to travel by plane.
c. How people usually travel in America.
d. How people spend their holidays.

## Part Two Listen Now

### Text One

#### I. Words and expressions

sip /sɪp/ *v.* 小口地喝，呷
congestion /kən'dʒestʃən/ *n.* 拥塞
whatsoever /ˌhwɒtsəʊ'evə/ *adj.* 任何的
commuter train 市郊往返列车
surface train 地面火车（相对地铁而言）

#### II. Listen to confirm or to adjust

*Listen and find out if your expectations are the same as or different from what you hear. If different, find the correct one or ones from **Make your prediction**.*

#### III. Listen and fill in the following blanks with the missing information.

1. How do people in Northfield go to work?
   By ____________, ____________, or on ______________.
2. Why do people in big cities go to work by public transportation instead of by car?
   Because ____________ a car is ______________.
3. How do people living in the suburbs of a big city go to work?
   By ______________________.
4. What can people do on a commuter train?

Read ______________, sip ________________, get ready for the _________________, use __________________ and talk ________________.

5. How large is Minneapolis?

   It is a ______________________________ city.

6. How much time does it take to go by car from Northfield to Minneapolis when traffic is good?

   About _________________ minutes.

7. If you leave Northfield at 7:00, at what time can you reach Minneapolis?

   At _______________.

## IV. Listen and decide whether the following statements are true (T) or false (F). If the statement is false, write the correction after it.

**Example:** The speaker lives far away from where he works. (F)

Correction: He lives three or four miles away.

1. In a big city like New York, people prefer to take subway because it's very quick. *T* ☐ *F* ☐
2. Freeways in big cities tend to be busy. *T* ☐ *F* ☐
3. A round trip ticket on the commuter train costs more than $20. *T* ☐ *F* ☐
4. Minneapolis doesn't have good public transportation. *T* ☐ *F* ☐
5. Many people take a bus to work from Northfield to Minneapolis. *T* ☐ *F* ☐

# Text Two

## I. Words and expressions

explore /ɪk'splɔː/ *v.* 探索；考察
compartment /kəm'pɑːtmənt/ *n.* 卧车包房
cramped /kræmpt/ *adj.* 狭窄的；受限制的
stiff /stɪf/ *adj.* 僵直的；不灵活的
like /laɪk/ *adv.* (口语)差不多；接近
freight train 货运列车
special promotions 特价推销

Greyhound Lines 灰狗巴士线（“灰狗”为美国一长途汽车公司名）
South Dakota /saʊθ də'kəʊtə/ 南达科他州（美国）
Seattle /sɪ'ætl/ 西雅图（美国港市）

## II. Listen to confirm or to adjust

*Listen and find out if your expectations are the same as or different from what you hear. If different, find the correct one or ones from* ***Make your prediction****.*

## III. Listen and choose the best answer to each question you hear.

1. a. By car.
   b. By bus.
   c. By train.
   d. By plane.
2. a. Because she lives quite near.
   b. Because no plane is available.
   c. Because they can enjoy the views along the way.
   d. Because it is safe to drive a car.
3. a. Fewer than 3 days.
   b. More than 3 days.
   c. 7 days.
   d. More than 7 days.
4. a. To travel by bus.
   b. To travel by car.
   c. To travel by train.
   d. To travel by plane.
5. a. It is uncomfortable.
   b. It is dirty.
   c. It is dangerous.
   d. It is time-consuming.

## IV. Listen and Fill in the following blanks with the missing information.

1. Prof. Bodman works at ___________.
2. He prefers to travel in ___________ because he has a ________-month vacation.

3. The American national system of superhighways was completed in the ________________.

4. Compared with the bus or airplane travel, the train travel is more ____________________.

5. Students and foreign visitors like to travel by bus because some bus companies like Greyhound Lines offer ______________________ and ____________________________.

## Part Three Look at This

**美国的交通运输**

在以上的采访中，Bodman 教授提到了美国人出游经常自己驾车或者乘飞机。他们喜欢自己驾车出游是因为美国的道路系统四通八达，且美国人口远远少于中国，因而道路相对比较畅通。另外，美国户均轿车拥有率相当高。美国的航空业很发达，坐飞机快捷便利，因而是美国人出远门的首选方式。在 ***Here's More*** 部分，大家将更多地了解美国的交通运输。

## Part Four Here's More

### Exercise

*I. In this part, you will hear 3 paragraphs. Please choose one of the following topics to match each of the paragraphs you hear.*

| | |
|---|---|
| A. Air Travel | 1. ________________ |
| B. Public Transportation | 2. ________________ |
| C. Carpools | 3. ________________ |

*II. Listen again and answer the following questions.*

1. What do many people ride to work from the outlying regions into the city like New York?

_______________________________________________________________

2. After they get off the trains, how do they usually go back home?

_______________________________________________________________

3. In major cities, how are different bus routes differentiated from one another?

_______________________________________________

4. If you'd like to have a plane ticket reservation changed, what do you have to do?

_______________________________________________

5. Do different airlines offer the same price for flights to the same destination?

_______________________________________________

6. How can you normally get a cheaper plane ticket?

_______________________________________________

7. What are carpools?

_______________________________________________

8. What is the advantage of carpooling in some large cities?

_______________________________________________

# Unit 5 Transportation and Traveling (Continued)

## Part One Before You Listen

### I. Think and answer

1. How do most people go traveling in China? Why?
2. What is the difference between a business travel and a leisure travel?
3. When do people usually go traveling?
4. Do you think people of different ages travel in the same way?

### II. Make your prediction

*Browse through all the information offered in this unit and predict the main idea of Text One and Text Two by choosing from a, b, c and d. You may choose more than one answer to indicate your prediction.*

**Text One**

a. Different ways to go to the same place.
b. Differences in ways of travelling and pricing.
c. Different plane fares and reasons.
d. Different attitudes towards traveling.

**Text Two**

a. People at different ages or with different occupations do different kinds of traveling.

b. People with different income go traveling to different places.

c. Old people like going to the South to escape the coldness in winter.

d. Young people like traveling all the year round.

## Part Two Listen Now

### Text One

#### I. Words and expressions

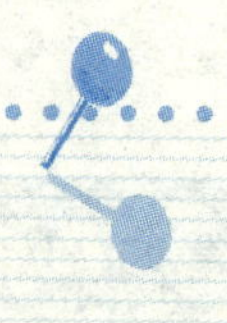

monopoly /mə'nɒpəlɪ/ *n.* 垄断(权); 专营(权)

in advance 提前

#### II. Listen to confirm or to adjust

*Listen and find out if your expectations are the same as or different from what you hear. If different, pick the correct one or ones from **Make your prediction**.*

#### III. Listen and answer the following questions.

1. Airplane travel in China is cheaper than that in the United States, but in China people still prefer to travel by train. Why?

   ______________________________

2. How can you buy a cheaper plane ticket if you want to travel from Minneapolis to New York?

   ______________________________

3. Which is farther away from Minneapolis, Rapid City or New York?

   ______________________________

4. Which costs you more, flying from Minneapolis to Rapid City or to New York? Why?

   ______________________________

## IV. Listen and decide whether the following statements are true (T) or false (F).

1. Unlike Chinese people, Americans travel a lot more by car and by plane. *T* ☐ *F* ☐
2. There isn't much difference between booking a plane ticket two months in advance and booking one week in advance. *T* ☐ *F* ☐
3. The more passengers traveling on a certain route, the more expensive the plane ticket is. *T* ☐ *F* ☐

# Text Two

## I. Words and expressions

resort /rɪˈzɔːt/ *n.* 度假地，游览胜地
destination /ˌdestɪˈneɪʃən/ *n.* 目的地
alumni /əˈlʌmnaɪ/ *n.* （复）校友
sponsor /ˈspɒnsə/ *v.* 赞助
miniature /ˈmɪnɪətʃə/ *adj.* 小型的，微型的
Florida /ˈflɔːrɪdə/ 佛罗里达州（美国）
leisure travel 休闲旅游
Labor Day （美国、加拿大的）劳工节（九月的第一个星期一）
Independence Day 美国独立纪念日（七月四日）
Easter 复活节（在三月或四月，每年过春分月圆后第一个星期日）
make sense 是明智的
the boy/girl scouts 男/女童子军
Thanksgiving 感恩节（十一月的最后一个星期四）
Spring Break 春假（三月底或四月初）
club together 和他人共同担负费用
Cornell Alumni University 康奈尔成人大学

## II. Listen to confirm or to adjust

*Listen and find out if your expectations are the same as or different from what you hear. If different, find the correct one or ones from **Make your prediction**.*

## III. Listen and fill in the blanks with the phrases given in the following box.

| | | |
|---|---|---|
| during the week | during the summer | during the winter |
| over Labor Day | over Independence Day | over Easter |
| during a paid vacation | at Christmas | at Thanksgiving |
| at Spring Break | | |

| Activities | When do they take place? |
|---|---|
| Business travel | 1. ______________ |
| Leisure travel | 2. ______________ |
| Children's summer camps | 3. ______________ |
| College students' travel | 4. ______________ |
| Educational travel | 5. ______________ |
| Retired people traveling south | 6. ______________ |

## IV. Listen and choose the best answer to each question you hear.

1. a. At weekends.
   b. On weekdays.
   c. On Labor Day.
   d. On Independence Day.

2. a. One week.
   b. One month.
   c. Two weeks.
   d. Two months.

3. a. Fishing and boating.
   b. Swimming.
   c. Camping.
   d. Hunting.

4. a. Boys and girls.
   b. All kinds of people.
   c. People who have kids.
   d. Young men and women.

5. a. By car.
   b. By plane.
   c. By ship.
   d. By train.

6. a. While you travel, you can teach.
   b. While you travel, you can take a course.

c. While you travel, you can visit some universities.
d. While you travel, you can meet your former schoolmates.

7. a. Rich people.
b. Poor people.
c. Retired people.
d. Sick people.

8. a. A bedroom.
b. A bathroom.
c. A kitchen.
d. A tiny hotel.

## Part Three Look at This

### 美国的节假日

无论是在美国还是中国，谈到出门旅游免不了要涉及节假日，因为节假日让人们有充裕的时间去游玩。在以上的采访中，Bodman 教授就提到了美国的数个节假日，如Labor Day，Independence Day，Easter，Thanksgiving，Christmas，Spring Break等。

美国共有十个公共节假日，它们是：

1. New Year's Day (January 1st)
2. Martin Luther King Day (the third Monday in January)
3. President's Day (the third Monday in February)
4. Memorial Day (the last Monday in May)
5. Independence Day (July 4th)
6. Labor Day (the first Monday in September)
7. Columbus Day (the second Monday in October)
8. Veterans Day (November 11th)
9. Thanksgiving Day (the fourth Thursday in November)
10. Christmas (December 25th)

在以上这十个节假日中，美国人最重视的要数感恩节和圣诞节了。事实上美国人更青睐感恩节。在感恩节到来前，你不需要去买礼物和别人交换，也不需要去装饰圣诞树，而可以轻松愉快地和家人团聚。

除了以上这十个公共节假日，美国还有许多五花八门的节日，如：

1. Valentine's Day (February 14th)
2. St. Patrick's Day (March 17th)
3. Professional Secretaries Day (Wednesday of the last full week in April)
4. Mother's Day (the second Sunday in May)
5. Father's Day (the third Sunday in June)
6. Parents' Day (the fourth Sunday in July)
7. Grandparents Day (the first Sunday after Labor Day)
8. Boss's Day (October 16th)
9. Halloween (the night of October 31st)
10. April Fools' Day (April 1st)
11. Groundhog Day (February 2nd)
12. Flag Day (June 14th)

在 ***Here's More*** 部分，大家将听到六个美国公共节假日的介绍，即：Martin Luther King Day, President's Day, Memorial Day, Labor Day, Columbus Day 和 Veterans Day。

## Part Four Here's More

### Exercise

*You will hear an introduction of six American public holidays. Listen three times and fill in the following blanks with the missing information.*

**1. Martin Luther King Day**

Martin Luther King Day was the first new public holiday to be implemented in the USA ____________________ and actually came into effect in 1986. There were no ______________________ or ceremonies, but the holiday was an opportunity for the media to remind people of how Martin Luther King struggled to reshape the __________________________ towards black people and in the end, how he paid the ultimate sacrifice for being prepared to speak out on the issue. Schools also use the commemoration as a __________________________ about the history of slavery and prejudice, and the life and work of this great man.

**2. President's Day**

The origins of this holiday ___________________ are that the birthdays of George Washington and Abraham Lincoln were on the __________ and __________ February respectively. With Washington being the ________________ of the USA and Lincoln the president at the time of the ________________, they had been ________________ for holidays to commemorate their birth.

In ________, however, President Richard Nixon ________ that the two separate holidays should be __________ and __________ by a one-day holiday in February called President's Day to ____________ not only the __________ of Washington and Lincoln, but ______________ through history.

**3. Memorial Day**

One of the ________ public holidays, Memorial Day is held to commemorate those who ________________ fighting in the American Civil War. Initially called ________________, the main remembrance ceremony ________ ________ in the city of Waterloo in New York.

**4. Labor Day**

Labor Day is a public holiday ____________ to the social and economic achievements of ________. It was proposed in ________ in New York by the Central Labor Union and has been ________________ ever since.

**5. Columbus Day**

Rather more controversial is the celebration of the ________________ of islands off the coast of America in 1492 by one Christopher Columbus, which some say, ________ the European ____________ of the Americas.

Suffice to say, many ________________ (Indian Tribes) are not too ______________ the fact that the American nation sees fit to celebrate some European mercenary with a __________ of direction claiming to have discovered a __________ which their ancestors ______________ on for thousands of years.

**6. Veterans Day**

Veterans Day is held ______________ those Americans who lost their lives fighting for their country. In 1921 an unknown American soldier ________ in the First World War was ________ in Arlington National Cemetery. This site, on a hillside __________ the Potomac River and the city of Washington, became the ______________ of reverence for American's veterans. ________ occurred earlier in England and France, where an unknown soldier was buried in ______________ highest place of honor: in England, Westminster Abbey, and in ________, the Arc de Triomphe. These ceremonies all took place on __________, giving universal recognition to the celebrated ending of ____________ fighting at 11.00 a.m., 11th November, __________, the day which ______________________ as Armistice Day.

Armistice Day officially _____________________________ in America in ____________ by a resolution of Congress and became a _________________ 12 years later.

In 1954, Congress was __________________________ an occasion to honor all those who had served America in all wars, _________________________ was equally preserved by those who fought in World War II. President Eisenhower __________ __________ proclaiming November 11th as Veterans Day.

The Focal point for official __________________________ on Veterans Day continues to be at the Tomb of the Unknowns at Arlington Cemetery. At ________ on November 11th, a combined color guard representing all _________________ executes Present Arms at the tomb. A Presidential wreath is _____________ and a bugler plays.

# Unit 6

# Marriage and Family

## Part One Before You Listen

### I. Think and answer

1. At what age do boys and girls around you begin to date?
2. What is the most important thing that you will take into consideration when you choose your girlfriend or boyfriend?
3. Before you get married, what must you do?
4. After you have children, how will you nurture them?

### II. Make your prediction

*Browse through all the information offered in this unit and predict the main idea of Text One and Text Two by choosing from a, b, c and d. You may choose more than one answer to indicate your prediction.*

#### Text One

a. Boyfriends and girlfriends.
b. Places where people date.
c. Dating and choosing boy- or girlfriends.
d. The age at which people begin to date.

#### Text Two

a. Marriage license.

b. Marriage and child-raising.
c. Wedding ceremony.
d. Expense on a wedding ceremony.

# Part Two Listen Now

## Text One

### I. Words and expressions

awareness /əˈweənɪs/ *n.* 意识；认识
gravitate /ˈgrævɪteɪt/ *v.* 被吸引而逐渐移向
exclusive /ɪkˈskluːsɪv/ *adj.* 专用的；独家的
steady /ˈstedɪ/ *adj.* 稳定的
underestimate /ˌʌndərˈestɪmeɪt/ *v.* 低估
Caucasian /kɔːˈkeɪzɪən/ *n.* 白种人
hang out 闲荡
vice versa 反过来(也是这样)

### II. Listen to confirm or to adjust

*Listen and find out if your predictions are the same as or different from what you hear. If different, find the correct one or ones from* ***Make your prediction****.*

### III. Listen and decide whether the following statements are true (T) or false (F).

1. In a traditional sense, dating means groups of boys and groups of girls "hang out" together. *T* ☐ *F* ☐
2. To date means one boy and one girl who gravitate towards each other spend some exclusive time together. *T* ☐ *F* ☐
3. When a boy at the age of 10 or 11 says he's "going out" with his date, he really means they go out together. *T* ☐ *F* ☐

4. Whether the two dating partners can really go out together largely depends on whether they are able to drive. *T* ☐ *F* ☐
5. Regardless of age, racial, economic, educational or social background, the appearance plays an important role when people choose their spouses. *T* ☐ *F* ☐

## IV. Listen and answer the following questions.

1. Does the traditional sense of dating apply to the present dating practice?

_______________________________________________

2. How did the interviewee's son "date" when he was 10 or 11?

_______________________________________________

3. When the son said "We're just going out," what did he basically mean?

_______________________________________________

4. How do you understand "to date basically means to have independence"?

_______________________________________________

5. What is very important for the dating couples according to the interviewee?

_______________________________________________

6. Where can people usually meet similar people?

_______________________________________________

# Text Two

## I. Words and expressions

syphilis /ˈsɪfɪlɪs/ *n.* 梅毒
AIDS /eɪdz/ *n.* Acquired Immune Deficiency Syndrome 艾滋病(获得性免疫缺损综合征)
minister /ˈmɪnɪstə/ *n.* 牧师
register /ˈredʒɪstə/ *v.* 登记；注册
resourcefulness /rɪˈsɔːsfʊlnɪs/ *n.* 机智，有办法
obedient /əʊˈbiːdɪənt/ *adj.* 顺从的；孝顺的
disobedient /ˌdɪsəˈbiːdjənt/ *adj.* 不顺从的，不听话的
self-reliant /ˌselfrɪˈlaɪənt/ *adj.* 自力更生的，自立的
Justice of the Peace 兼理一般司法事务的地方官(在美国还有证婚权)

marriage license 结婚证书
sexual intercourse 性交
on average 平均
in the neighborhood of 大约
stand up to 抵抗，对抗
talk back 回嘴，顶嘴

## II. Listen to confirm or to adjust

*Listen and find out if your predictions are the same as or different from what you hear. If different, find the correct one or ones from **Make your prediction**.*

## III. Listen and choose the best answer to each of the following questions.

1. Where in the United States can people get a marriage license?
   a. From the national government.
   b. From the state government.
   c. From the county government.
   d. From the provincial government.

2. Before the couple fill out the marriage license form, what do they have to do?
   a. Go to a minister of a church.
   b. Go to a judge.
   c. Take blood test.
   d. Register at the county.

3. If a couple have never had sexual intercourse, how do they end their marriage?
   a. They should get divorced.
   b. They don't need to get divorced.
   c. They should go to register first.
   d. They won't be allowed to get divorced.

4. On average how much do a newly married couple spend on a typical wedding?
   a. $160,000.
   b. $2,000.
   c. $20,000.
   d. $16,000.

5. Who pay(s) more for a wedding in American society?
   a. The parents of the groom.

b. The parents of the bride.
c. The grandparents of the groom.
d. The grandparents of the bride.

6. What is the most important thing that American parents emphasize when they raise children?
   a. Resourcefulness.
   b. Talking back.
   c. Independence.
   d. Depending on their parents.

## IV. Listen and fill in the following blanks with the missing information.

1. The marriages in the United States are governed by the ________________.
2. The authority to marry a couple is usually a ___________ of a ____________ or some kind of a ______________ leader.
3. It is not _____________ to get divorced in the United States.
4. A nice wedding can be very _____________ in America.
5. A typical age for men and women to get married in America is around ______ to _______ years old.
6. American parents encourage _____________________ and ________________.
7. In Asia, children seem to be more ________________.

# Part Three Look at This

**婚姻和婚礼习俗**

在以上的采访中，Leming 教授谈到了美国人的约会、择偶、婚姻、婚礼等，我们可从中了解一些美国人在这方面的风俗习惯。

在 ***Here's More*** 里，我们选择了两篇关于美国人的婚姻和婚礼习俗的短文，以便让大家进一步扩展这方面的知识。

## Part Four Here's More

### Exercise One

*Listen and decide whether the following statements are true (T) or false (F).*

1. In the United States parents usually help their children find their wives or husbands. *T* ☐ *F* ☐
2. Ideally love is a prerequisite for being able to live happily. *T* ☐ *F* ☐
3. Values such as economic support and the opportunity to have children are not important at all. *T* ☐ *F* ☐

### Exercise Two

*Listen and fill in the following blanks with the missing information.*

1. Nowadays it is unnecessary for a young man to ask his would-be father-in-law for permission to ____________ his daughter, but he still wants him to approve of their __________.
2. At a simple wedding reception, ______________________ are offered in the church, while at an elaborate one there will be a large _________________ dinner held at a _________________, and after the dinner there will be a ______________ with a _____________ orchestra.
3. If you are invited to a wedding reception, you are supposed to give ________________.
4. People can opt to get married either in a ________________ ceremony or in a ____________ one.
5. Priests, ministers and rabbis have the right to ____________ people.
6. It is said that every bride at her wedding should wear something _________, something _________, something _______________ and something ____________.
7. To see the bride in her wedding dress before the ceremony is _____________ as bad luck for the ____________.
8. The rice thrown at _________________________________ after the ceremony signals fertility.

# Unit 7

# Divorce

## Part One Before You Listen

### I. Think and answer

1. Do you think these days there are more people getting divorced than a few years ago?
2. How do you look at those who get divorced?
3. Do you think the divorce rate will continue rising or decrease? Why?

### II. Make your prediction

*Browse through all the information offered in this unit and predict the main idea of Text One and Text Two by choosing from a, b, c and d. You may choose more than one answer to indicate your prediction.*

**Text One**

a. High divorce rate and its causes.
b. The divorce rate is ever-increasing.
c. People get divorced for very trivial things.
d. Scared by the high divorce rate, many people choose not to get married.

**Text Two**

a. The divorce rate has decreased sharply.
b. Divorce is always associated with stigma.
c. People's attitude toward divorce has changed and so has the divorce rate.
d. It is inexplicable why divorce rate keeps changing.

## Part Two Listen Now

### Text One

### I. Words and expressions

status /ˈstætəs/ *n.* 状况
longitudinal /ˌlɒndʒɪˈtjuːdɪnəl/ *adj.* 纵观的
alcoholic /ˌælkəˈhɒlɪk/ *n.* 嗜酒者
individualistic /ˈɪndɪˌvɪdjʊəˈlɪstɪk/ *adj.* 个人的
abuse /əˈbjuːz/ *n.* 虐待，伤害
alcoholism /ˈælkəhɒlɪzəm/ *n.* 酗酒
involvement /ɪnˈvɒlvmənt/ *n.* 卷入，介入，参与
nurture /ˈnɜːtʃə/ *v.* 养育，培育
break up 结束；解散
soul mate 意气相投的人；心心相印的伙伴
Hallmark greeting card (生日、节假日等场合)致亲友的贺卡
No-Fault Divorce Law 无过错离婚法
societally speaking 从社会的角度来说

### II. Listen to confirm or to adjust

*Listen and find out if your expectations are the same as or different from what you hear. If different, find the correct one or ones from **Make your prediction**.*

### III. Listen and choose the best answer to each of the following questions.

1. How do you understand that the United States has a divorce rate of 50%?
   a. Half of the couples who get married within a certain year get divorced in that exact year.
   b. Half of the couples who get married within a certain year will get divorced sooner or later in their lifetime.
   c. Half of the married couples will get divorced.

d. Half of the married couples or people who will get married will finally get divorced.

2. What is the current trend of the divorce rate according to Michelle?
   a. It keeps rising.
   b. It is now steady.
   c. It has decreased in a way.
   d. It is difficult to predict.

3. Sociologically speaking, what is the common cause for a marriage to break up?
   a. The reasons for divorce are varied.
   b. The communication problem is the main cause.
   c. The husband or wife is an alcoholic.
   d. There is an increasing emphasis placed on individualism.

4. What did Michelle marry for?
   a. Financial support.
   b. Children.
   c. Emotional needs.
   d. An unknown reason.

## IV. Listen and fill in the following blanks with the missing information.

1. In any given year, there have been __________ to __________ getting divorced per __________ thousand ________________ since the mid 1980s.
2. In fact the divorce rate is ________________ in the United States.
3. The two factors that have largely contributed to the high divorce rate in the United States:
   a. More emphasis on having only one other person __________ every single one of the __________________________.
   b. The ________________ Divorce Law issued in ____________.

# Text Two

## I. Words and expressions

stigma /ˈstɪgmə/ *n.* 耻辱，羞辱

stereotype /ˈsterɪəʊtaɪp/ *n.* 陈规，老套，模式化的见解 *v.* 把……模式化；用僵硬的态度对待……

norm /nɔːm/ *n.* 规范，准则

## II. Listen to confirm or to adjust

*Listen and find out if your expectations are the same as or different from what you hear. If different, find the correct one or ones from **Make your prediction**.*

## III. Listen and fill in the following blanks with the missing information.

1. Now __________ of the students in the interviewee's class are willing to admit that they are __________ by divorce.
2. But 50 years ago, ________ or ________ of the students asked would be willing to say so.
3. Though less ___________ is attached to ___________, people still hold a ___________ attitude toward it.
4. In 1973, the divorce rate _________________________; in the mid 1980s it reached its ____________. After that it has _____________________________, and maybe even ____________.

## IV. Listen and decide whether the following statements are true (T) or false (F).

1. According to Michelle, when divorce was socially acceptable, more and more married couples got divorced. *T* ☐ *F* ☐
2. If you got divorced in the past, you used to be viewed as a failure. *T* ☐ *F* ☐
3. As there is less stigma on people who have been divorced, most people now go into divorce situations lightly. *T* ☐ *F* ☐
4. The fact that more and more women have gained economic independence from men in a way contributes to the high divorce rate. *T* ☐ *F* ☐

# Look at This

### 采访的篇章特点以及怎样听懂迂回曲折的回答

采访的总体框架是问答，它也具有会话的特点。采访人在采访中起着话题导向作用，他/她有时用陈述句引出话题，有时对所谈的内容作一些评论、归纳或发问等使谈话继续，有时则通过这些方式引领谈话从一个话题转到另一个话题。而被采访人回答问题或接过采访人的话题时，有时直截了当、简单明了地回答或阐述，有时则迂回间接或洋洋洒洒地说上一大段。对直截了当、简单明了的回答听者比较容易抓住，而迂回间接、洋洋洒洒的回答却要求听者认真仔细地揣摩出要点。在Text One里，Michelle 回答两个问题时说 But it's very difficult to measure 和 that's a difficult question to answer，听到这样的回答，我们可以预测被采访人接下来的话会比较长，不是简单明了、直截了当的那种。碰到这种情况时，我们可以通过关注讲话中使用的信号词和转变话题的过渡句来判断讲话的要点。所以在听采访时，我们需要注意以下几点：

1. 听清楚采访人的话或问题至关重要。在采访中采访人处于主导位置，引领并把握着整个采访的方向。例如：

**Interviewer:** So you pay a lot of attention to dinner. Can you tell me, on average, how many hours do you spend cooking dinner?

在这里，So you pay a lot of attention to dinner 起到了归纳总结的作用，而它后面的问句则起到了承上启下的作用，我们可以预测接下来的话题是花在做饭上的时间。

所以被采访人会讲些什么很大程度上取决于采访人。采访人决定话题，被采访人提供细节，展开话题。

2. 关注被采访人的回答是直截了当还是迂回曲折。如果是后一种，我们可以借助信号词和承上启下的过渡句来归纳出要点。例如：

**Interviewer:** What do you think are the common factors that cause a marriage to break up?

**Michelle:** Um...that's a difficult question to answer <u>because everyone will look at their own situation.</u> Uh...and say, uh...you know, I got divorced because um...my husband was an alcoholic or because uh...we had communication problems or because I was just unhappy. And all of these are very, seem like very individualistic uh...reasons for divorcing.

**Interviewer:** So people get divorced for different reasons, all very individualistic.

**Michelle:** Yes. <u>But I think if we look at the whole picture, uh...sociologically speaking,</u> uh...we can take these individual stories, you know, if there's abuse, if there's alcoholism, if there's a communication problem... whatever the reasons might be, and look at it from an American sociological point of view, what we see is an increasing emphasis placed on individualism, uh...a lack of emphasis placed on community and family involvement in your marriage. *Uh...so you know, 150 years ago,* in the, even in the United States you had a lot more influence from your parents and other family members in the community about whom you marry. And you got married for very practical reasons.

| | |
|---|---|
| | Economically women needed someone to provide for them; men needed to marry somebody who could provide children and nurturing, and domestic service. |
| **Interviewer:** | That's not true any more. |
| **Michelle:** | Ya, *when I got married,* I didn't need to get married for financial reasons because I have a separate career of my own and have financial independence from my husband. So today we have an increased emphasis on emotions. And you marry somebody because you are in love with them. And you find you're a soul mate and it's all very nice and on the back of the Hallmark greeting card. Uh...and so of course what happens is, the more emphasis you place on having only one other person meet every single one of your emotional needs which by the way is impossible, the more likely you are to become disappointed. And you place that one on top of the fact that it's easy to get a divorce in this country. |
| **Interviewer:** | So you mean it's more difficult to meet the emotional needs than financial ones. |
| **Michelle:** | It's doubtless. Especially since 1973, with the No-Fault Divorce Law, you take all these things in consideration. Uh...societally speaking, it helps explain why people are more likely to get divorced than they used to be. |

以上这段话有三层意思：1) 表面上看，离婚的原因多种多样。2) 从社会学的角度来看，这是个人主义的不断膨胀引起的。而妇女拥有独立的经济地位、为了爱而结婚则是一个具体的例子。3) 1973年颁布的无过错离婚法对高离婚率起了推波助澜的作用。

以上三处划线部分是展开三个要点、点出话题的部分。而斜体部分引出支撑第二个要点的具体例子：150年前和现今的对比。如果在听时能抓住这些词句，并能意识到话题的转换，那么领会要点是不难的。关于领会要点，我们在第8单元的***Look at This***中将更详细地展开探讨。

## Part Four Here's More

### Exercise One

*You will hear some questions asked by different interviewers. Listen to each question and write down a few words to indicate the topic that will be talked about later.*

**Example:**

Interviewer: So you swapped courses and began to talk more in class. Was there anything else that the counselor suggested?

Topic: The counselor's suggestions.

**Topics**

1. ____________________
2. ____________________
3. ____________________
4. ____________________
5. ____________________
6. ____________________
7. ____________________
8. ____________________
9. ____________________
10. ____________________

## Exercise Two

*I. Listen to two excerpts from an interview and fill in the following blanks with the missing information.*

1. **Detailed:** Responsible for the ____________ of the passengers and the ____________ of the plane and passengers.

   **Generalized:** Responsible for ____________.

2. **Disadvantages of the career:** Not ____________; can be ____________; affects ____________.

   **Advantages of the career:** ____________; never ____________.

*II. Listen again and write down the transitional words or transitional sentences in the two excerpts which lead the topics from the detailed responsibility to the generalized one and from the disadvantages of the career to the advantages.*

1. ____________________
2. ____________________

# Unit 8

# Divorce (Continued)

## Part One Before You Listen

### I. Think and answer

1. What do you think could cause the divorce rate to stay steady or decrease a little?
2. What is the most important thing to keep marriage going?
3. What can be considered essential when you choose a spouse?

### II. Make your prediction

*Browse through all the information offered in this unit and predict the main idea of Text One and Text Two by choosing from a, b, c and d. You may choose more than one answer to indicate your prediction.*

**Text One**

a. How to keep marriage going.
b. How to look at the high divorce rate falling a little bit.
c. How to combat the problem of high divorce rate.
d. How to get along with your children.

**Text Two**

a. Whether you are happy or not depends on when you get married.
b. If you don't know how to deal with conflict, you'd better not to get married.
c. Don't marry anyone who is 10 years older than you.
d. There are many factors that can lead to divorce.

## Part Two Listen Now

### Text One

#### I. Words and expressions

backlash /ˈbæklæʃ/ *n.* (对重大事件的)强烈反应，对抗性反应
combat /ˈkɒmbæt/ *v.* 与……战斗；与……斗争
therapist /ˈθerəpɪst/ *n.* (特定治疗法的)治疗专家
abusive /əˈbjuːsɪv/ *adj.* 骂人的；辱骂性的
intimate /ˈɪntɪmət/ *adj.* 亲密的；密切的
setting /ˈsetɪŋ/ *n.* 背景；环境
productive /prəʊˈdʌktɪv/ *adj.* 多产的；丰饶的
fall apart 破碎；破裂
figure out 理解；想出

#### II. Listen to confirm or to adjust

*Listen and find out if your expectations are the same as or different from what you hear. If different, find the correct one or ones from* ***Make your prediction****.*

#### III. Listen twice and answer the following questions.

1. According to Michelle, why has the high divorce rate begun to decrease?
   a. ______________________________
   b. ______________________________
2. What is the important question to be considered when people go through a difficult marriage?
   ______________________________
3. Is divorce completely unnecessary according to Michelle?
   ______________________________

4. What questions should you consider when you evaluate your communication pattern?
   a. ______________________________
   b. ______________________________
   c. ______________________________
   d. ______________________________

5. What are the two extreme settings that the family could have?
   a. ______________________________
   b. ______________________________

6. What should you keep in mind according to Michelle?
   a. ______________________________
   b. ______________________________

## IV. Listen and decide whether the following statements are true (T) or false (F).

1. A lot of researchers are now beginning to understand why the high divorce rate is decreasing. T ☐ F ☐
2. Michelle's opinion of the decreasing divorce rate is the same as other researchers. T ☐ F ☐
3. Michelle thinks that divorce is not the only way to solve the marriage problem. T ☐ F ☐
4. Michelle believes what really counts in a marriage is the way you communicate with your spouse. T ☐ F ☐

# Text Two

## I. Words and expressions

engagement /ɪn'geɪdʒmənt/ *n.* 订婚；婚约
commitment /kə'mɪtmənt/ *n.* 承诺；承担的义务
sibling /'sɪblɪŋ/ *n.* 兄弟姐妹
institution /ˌɪnstɪ'tju:ʃən/ *n.* 制度；习俗
racial /'reɪʃəl/ *adj.* 种族的
ethnic /'eθnɪk/ *adj.* 种族的，民族的
prejudice /'predʒʊdɪs/ *n.* 偏见；歧视
cohabit /kəʊ'hæbɪt/ *v.* (未结婚者)同居
intimacy /'ɪntɪməsɪ/ *n.* 亲密；密切
end up 最后成为(处于)

## II. Listen to confirm or to adjust

*Listen and find out if your expectations are the same as or different from what you hear. If different, find the correct one or ones from **Make your prediction**.*

## III. Listen twice and fill in the following blanks with the missing information.

**You are more likely to get divorced,**

1. if you marry somebody before you are ______________________________;
2. if you marry somebody less than ______________________________;
3. if you marry somebody after you have been ______________________________;
4. if you have a history of a poor relationship with ______________________________;
5. if your parents got ______________________________;
6. if you have a very different ______________________________ from your partner;
7. if you cohabit with somebody ______________________________ and while you're living together, you have no ______________________________.

## IV. Listen and answer the questions you hear.

1. ______________________________
2. ______________________________
3. ______________________________
4. ______________________________

# Look at This

### 从被采访人的"长篇大论"中归纳要点

在采访中，被采访人经常会用长篇大论来回答某一个问题。在本单元中，被采访人Michelle就用比较长的篇幅回答了被问到的每一个问题。那么在听的时候，怎样取其要点呢？ **1）抓住一些标志性的词或词组。**比如在本单元Text One里，Michelle在回答时用了another possible reason这样的标志性词组从一个原因转到另一个原因，如果听的时候特别留意这样的词组，就能很快跟上她的思路，即：她刚才讲了第一个原因，接着要讲第二个原因了。**2) 应该从词义或句意来判断被采访人是否从一个要点转到了另一个。**比如 Text One 中 Michelle 谈到应该允许离婚存在，但当事人要三思而行，听者应该注意她是怎样从一层意思转到另一层意思的——她用 But if you're in a marriage where you're just unhappy and you can't figure out what's going on 作了一个转折。**3) 注意排比句之类。**在本单元的 Text Two 里，Michelle 在列举可能导致离婚的因素时用了排比句，听的时候抓住了这一系列排比句也就抓住了要点。

## Part Four Here's More

### Exercise

*Listen twice and write down the main points of each interviewee's answer.*

1. Programs to help reduce the stress:
   a. ____________________
   b. ____________________
   c. ____________________
2. Personal ways to help reduce the stress:
   a. ____________________
   b. ____________________
   c. ____________________
3. The kinds of kids who can do better:
   a. ____________________
   b. ____________________
   c. ____________________
4. The advantages that the machine has:
   a. ____________________
   b. ____________________
   c. ____________________

# Unit 9

# Teaching at High School and University

## Part One Before You Listen

### I. Think and answer

1. Do you want to be a teacher? Why?
2. What is required if you want to become a teacher in your country?
3. In your opinion, what is a good teacher like?
4. Does a teacher earn a lot in your country?
5. Which is more challenging, to teach in a middle school or in a college?

### II. Make your prediction

*Browse through all the information offered in this unit and predict the main idea of Text One and Text Two by choosing from a, b, c and d. You may choose more than one answer to indicate your prediction.*

**Text One**

a. School teachers' and university professors' work.
b. School teachers' and university professors' pay.
c. School teachers' and university professors' qualifications.
d. Reasons why some people want to choose teaching as their career.

### Text Two

a. Evaluation of teachers' work.

b. The largest challenges a teacher may face.

c. An unproven theory about how to be a good schoolteacher or a good college professor.

d. A teaching and learning system.

## Part Two Listen Now

### Text One

#### I. Words and expressions

schoolteacher /ˈskuːlˌtiːtʃə/ *n.* (中小学)教师
certificate /səˈtɪfɪkət/ *n.* 证明书；执照
attain /əˈteɪn/ *v.* 获得
Ph. D. *abbr.* (Doctor of Philosophy) 哲学博士；博士
profession /prəʊˈfeʃən/ *n.* (尤指从事脑力劳动或需要专门训练的)职业
welfare /ˈwelfeə/ *n.* 福利
credit /ˈkredɪt/ *n.* 学分
likewise /ˈlaɪkwaɪz/ *adv.* 同样地
service-oriented /ˈsɜːvɪs ˈɔːrɪentɪd/ *adj.* 着重(为他人)服务的

#### II. Listen to confirm or to adjust

*Listen and find out if your expectations are the same as or different from what you hear. If different, find the correct one or ones from **Make your prediction**.*

#### III. Listen and choose the best answer to complete each of the following sentences.

1. ________, a teaching certificate is not necessary.

a. For a junior high school teacher

b. For an elementary school teacher

c. For a college professor

d. For a senior high school teacher

2. In the US, a college professor's salary is _______ a schoolteacher's.

a. a little higher than

b. much higher than

c. a little lower than

d. exactly the same as

3. Professor Solid feels _______ to explain why some people choose to be a teacher.

a. annoyed

b. glad

c. sorry

d. uncomfortable

4. Some people want to be a teacher because _______.

a. they want a challenging life

b. they can have a good salary

c. they love to work in the paying industry

d. they are interested in working with people

## IV. Listen and fill in the following blanks with the missing information.

1. In the US, in order to get a teaching certificate, a candidate must have ________________ ____________ and complete __________________. The program includes professional courses and ___________________.
2. According to Professor Solid, in the college, a teacher without a Ph. D. can still be valuable if he/she ___________________________.
3. Either in a public school or a college, a brand-new graduate without teaching experience must _________________ first. Then, after some years' teaching, he/she can expect _________________ in pay.
4. In the US, compared to some other professions, teaching ________________________. However, some people are still interested in teaching. According to Professor Solid, these people are usually service-oriented, ________________________ and are not so ________________________________.

## Text Two

### I. Words and expressions

assessment /ə'sesmənt/ *n.* 评估　(assess /ə'ses/ *v.* 评估)
evaluation /ɪ'væljʊ'eɪʃən/ *n.* 评价　(evaluate /ɪ'væljʊeɪt/ *v.* 评价)
passion /'pæʃən/ *n.* 激情，热情
enthusiastic /ɪn,θju:zɪ'æstɪk/ *adj.* 热情的，热烈的
enthusiasm /ɪn'θju:zɪæzəm/ *n.* 热情，积极性
methodology /,meθə'dɒlədʒɪ/ *n.* 方法论，研究方法
diversity /daɪ'vɜ:sətɪ/ *n.* 多样性
motivation /,məʊtɪ'veɪʃən/ *n.* 动机；动力
motivate /'məʊtɪveɪt/ *v.* 促动，激发

### II. Listen to confirm or to adjust

*Listen and find out if your expectations are the same as or different from what you hear. If different, find the correct one or ones from **Make your prediction**.*

### III. Listen and choose the best answer to each question you hear.

1. a. The existing theories.
   b. Other teachers' experience.
   c. His own teaching experience.
   d. Some unproven theories.

2. a. Evaluation and assessment.
   b. Different family backgrounds.
   c. Working with individuals and groups.
   d. Using different methodologies.

3. a. Professor Solid has been teaching for almost more than years.
   b. Professor Solid used to teach math and physics and science.
   c. Professor Solid thinks it more challenging to teach young learners than to teach young adults.

d. Professor Solid's current students are studying for the teaching certificate because all of them want to work in public schools.

4. a. Making them love teaching.
   b. Making them love what they teach.
   c. Making them understand teaching is also a science.
   d. Making them love their students.

## IV. Listen and fill in the following blanks with the missing information.

**Professor Solid's theory — 4 needs for those who want to be a good teacher:**

A. (1) ________________. It involves:
   1. Assisting learners creatively.
   2. Assessment.
   3. Evaluation.
   4. (2) ________________.
   5. Management.
   6. Giving grades.

B. Like (3) ________________.
   1. Have a passion for (4) ________________.
   2. Share the passion with young learners.

C. Like young people.
   1. If learners are children, teachers must like being with them and (5) ________________.
   2. If learners are (6) ________________, teachers must like (7) ________________ and understand who they are and where they are.

D. (8) ________________.
   1. (9) ________________ about themselves and their profession. In other words, they should (10) ________________.
   2. Be involved in teaching and share it with others.

   Conclusion: All the four needs must coexist and a good teacher will have (11) ________________ although he/she is not well paid.

**The largest challenges in Professor Solid's teaching career:**

A. At public school level:
   1. (12) ________________.
      Reasons:
      i. Public school education is free and compulsory.
      ii. Students from some backgrounds don't think (13) ________________.
   2. Meet various needs of students.
      Reason:
      i. Students have different (14) ________________.

B. At college level (especially when working with those majoring in teaching):

1. Show students (15) ____________________ to teaching.

   It involves:

   i. How to make teaching effective.

   ii. (16) ____________________.

## Part Three Look at This

### 美国的教育制度

1. 在美国，学校教育机构大致分为小学(primary school 或 elementary school)、中学(secondary school，包括junior high 和 high school)和大学(college 或 university)。除此之外，还有其他一些国家认可的教育机构，比如community college，junior college，ESL(English as a second language)school 以及 sports academy。请注意，在美国，公办学校称为public school，但在英国，public school是指收费学校或私立学校(英国公立学校叫state school 或 government school)，比如著名的Eton College(每个学生一年的费用可达22,500 英镑)就是一所public school。
2. 美国学生在进入大学前必须获得高中毕业文凭(high school diploma)。进入大学后，教学模式如下：
   1) 学生可以自选课程，包括主修课程(classes in the main area of study)和辅修课程(classes in other areas，如dance，theater 和 sports)。
   2) 学生上课的形式以听讲座(lecture)为主；但有时教授也会安排他们的助理为学生开设小课(small class)，专供学生就上课内容提问和讨论。
   3) 学生参加考试的形式各有不同，除传统的考试外，还有一些教授会让学生写论文(write a research paper)或完成一项任务(complete a task)，以此来代替考试。
3. 在美国，没有全国性的教育标准和规定(national standards or guides)，于是美国的教师必须自己选择教材，并制定教学计划。在课堂上，教师们要灌输给学生这样一种理念，即Don't believe anything unless you have experienced personally。于是，教师们须时刻留心，不让自己的看法影响或主导学生对事物的认识。

# Part Four Here's More

## Exercise

*You will listen to an introduction of American education system. Listen and fill in the following blanks with the missing information. (One word for each blank.)*

In America, students must finish (1) ________ years' primary and secondary education before going to a college or university. Most American children start school at (2) ________. The first year at school is called (3) ________. So primary school consisting of (4) ________ years actually starts from the second year which is considered as the first grade.

Compared with the primary school education, secondary education is longer, which is referred to as (5) ________ through (6) ________ grades. Having accomplished it, a student will be (7) ________ a certificate which to some extent ensures his/her qualification for higher education.

In the college or university, (8) ________ students have access to two kinds of degrees: a two-year degree (called an (9) ________ degree) and a four-year degree (called a bachelor's degree). Usually when a student finishes a two-year degree, he/she can continue the education for a bachelor's degree. Although most schools won't say no to those who haven't chosen their (10) ________, it is required that they must choose one by their second year at school.

For those who want to (11) ________ in a specific field, they can (12) ________ their education for a master's degree or a Ph.D. In many cases, they must have obtained a bachelor's degree in the related field. But there are still (13) ________, for example, when a person wants to pursue an (14) ________ degree. In detail, a master's degree is a two-year degree while a Ph.D. can take between three and (15) ________ years. In fact, the length of a doctorate degree is mostly determined by the chosen (16) ________, the student's (17) ________ and the selected (18) ________.

# Unit 10 Campus Life

## Part One Before You Listen

### I. Think and answer

1. Are you interested in most courses offered by your university? Do you find them useful to your future career?
2. What do you think of working part-time on campus or off campus? What kind of part-time job will you take if you have to? Why?
3. What are the advantages and negative side effects of doing part-time jobs?
4. What leisure activities do you usually go in for after class?
5. What's your opinion towards campus love?
6. What do you think of your school life?

### II. Make your prediction

*Browse through all the information offered in this unit and predict the main idea of Text One and Text Two by choosing from a, b, c and d. You may choose more than one answer to indicate your prediction.*

**Text One**

a. Courses taken in college.
b. After-class activities.
c. Sports and entertainment in college.
d. Part-time jobs.

### Text Two

a. Off-campus part-time jobs.
b. Future career preparations.
c. Four-year school life.
d. Love on campus.

## Part Two Listen Now

### Text One

#### I. Words and expressions

linguistic /lɪŋˈgwɪstɪk/ *adj.* 语言(学)的
collegian /kəˈliːdʒjən/ *n.* 大学(在校)生
St. Olaf College 圣欧勒夫学院(位于美国明尼苏达州)
Wisconsin /wɪsˈkɒnsɪn/ 威斯康星州(美国)
Milwaukee /mɪlˈwɔːkiː/ 密尔沃基(美国威斯康星州东南部港市)

#### II. Listen to confirm or to adjust

*Listen and find out if your expectations are the same as or different from what you hear. If different, find the correct one or ones from* ***Make your prediction****.*

#### III. Listen and complete the following table.

| | |
|---|---|
| **Name** | (1) ______________________ |
| **College** | (2) ______________________ |
| **Major** | (3) ______________________ |
| **Academic year** | (4) ______________________ |
| **Courses taken this semester** | Four courses; twelve times a week<br>(5) ______________________ |

| | |
|---|---|
| | (6) ________<br>(7) ________<br>(8) ________ |
| **After-class activities** | Go back to the dorm and (9) ________<br>(10) ________<br>Go out (11) ________<br>(12) ________ |
| **Part-time jobs** | Types: on campus<br>off campus: work as (13) ________<br>work at (14) ________<br>Purposes: (15) ________<br>(16) ________, including gas and<br>(17) ____ (18) ________ |

### IV. Listen and decide whether the following statements are true (T) or false (F).

1. The student being interviewed is an international student. *T* ☐ *F* ☐
2. Students in the university may go skiing or sleighing in winter because of the favorable weather condition. *T* ☐ *F* ☐
3. According to the student being interviewed, most students in the university work part-time. *T* ☐ *F* ☐
4. Working part-time is the only way students choose to pay for their tuition cost. *T* ☐ *F* ☐

## Text Two

### I. Words and expressions

Istanbul /ˌɪstænˈbuːl/ 伊斯坦布尔(土耳其西北部港市)
Turkey /ˈtɜːkɪ/ 土耳其

### II. Listen to confirm or to adjust

*Listen and find out if your expectations are the same as or different from what you hear. If different, find the correct one or ones from **Make your prediction**.*

## III. Listen and choose the best answer to each question you hear.

1. a. Go to movies.
   b. Go to dinner.
   c. Go dancing.
   d. Go for a coffee.

2. a. Freshman year.
   b. Sophomore year.
   c. Junior year.
   d. Senior year.

3. a. Hong Kong.
   b. Berlin.
   c. Istanbul.
   d. Turkey.

## IV. Listen and fill in the following blanks with the missing information.

1. Most students have boyfriends or girlfriends, but not serious in ____________________ ____________.
2. Looking back as a senior, the speaker thinks that ________________________________.
3. When the speaker first came to St. Olaf College, she was excited because ____ ______________________.
4. During the first semester of this year, the student went to Hong Kong to ______ __________________________ at ______________________________.

## Part Three Look at This

### 美国的高等教育

课文里 Rachel 所在的大学 St. Olaf College 是一所教会学校。美国人为他们的大学感到自豪，因为美国有着世界第一流的知名大学，如我们所熟悉的 Harvard University, Princeton University, Yale University, Massachusetts Institute of Technology, Stanford University, University of Pennsylvania 等。美国的大学可按不同的方法分类，这里我们将它们按照办学费用的来源分为两类：

1. 由州政府资助的公立院校。美国五十个州每个都有好几所乃至几十所公立大学，如Pennsylvania State University，Ohio State University，the University of California，the University of North Carolina 以及 the University of Texas 等都是州立大学。这些大学通常规模较大，可以就不同领域的学习颁发学位。州立大学一般本科都是四年制，为合格的毕业生颁发学士学位。与私立大学相比，这些公立大学最大的好处就是学费比较便宜，如果你是当地的居民，就更能享受优惠的价格。一些两年制的社区学院学费更是便宜。

2. 由个人或宗教团体创办的私立学校。美国高等院校目前有70%是私立的，而且办得最好的大学多数是私立的，美国常青藤盟校中的University of Pennsylvania（不同于Pennsylvania State University），Harvard University等都是举世闻名的私立学校。私立大学的学费较高。我们本单元所听采访中的学生就来自明尼苏达州的一所私立大学。

## Part Four Here's More

### Exercise

*You will hear a passage. Listen twice and answer the following questions.*

1. What are the two characteristics of state universities as far as academic fields are concerned according to the passage?

   ______________________________

2. What are the college entrance requirements in recent years?

   ______________________________

3. What kind of students can go to state universities without paying high tuition fees?

   ______________________________

4. Where do most university students live?

   ______________________________

# Unit 11

# Anna in Australia

## Part One Before You Listen

### I. Think and answer

1. What problems will a nonnative speaker in an Australian college usually have?
2. Is it easy for an overseas graduate to find a job in Australia?
3. How do you enlarge your vocabulary in English?
4. What do you know about people's nutritional habits in China and in Australia?
5. Why do a lot of people believe in having a proper breakfast?

### II. Make your prediction

*Browse through all the information offered in this unit and predict the main idea of Text One and Text Two by choosing from a, b, c and d. You may choose more than one answer to indicate your prediction.*

**Text One**

a. Anna's current job.
b. Anna's problems in applying for a visa.
c. Anna's problems in academic study.
d. Anna's advice to college students.

**Text Two**

a. How Anna found her first job.
b. How Anna improved her English.
c. A project Anna used to engage herself in.
d. Anna's plan for the future.

# Part Two Listen Now

## Text One

### I. Words and expressions

tertiary /ˈtɜːʃərɪ/ *adj.* 高等教育的
council /ˈkaʊnsəl/ *n.* 委员会
direction /dɪˈrekʃən/ *n.* 专业方向
dietician /ˌdaɪəˈtɪʃən/ *n.* 营养师
nutritionally /njuːˈtrɪʃənəlɪ/ *adv.* 在营养方面
swap /swɒp/ *v.* 交换
Associate Diploma （澳洲）两年制专科证书
nutritional science 营养学

### II. Listen to confirm or to adjust

*Listen and find out if your expectations are the same as or different from what you hear. If different, find the correct one or ones from* ***Make your prediction****.*

### III. Listen and complete the following table.

| Name | Anna Cherney |
|---|---|
| Status | Nonnative speaker in Australia |
| Graduation from college | (1) ______________ years ago |
| Degree | Associate Diploma |
| Major | (2) ______________________________ |
| Current employment | Working with (3) ______________________ |

## IV. Listen and write down the meaning of the following expressions according to the interview.

1. An example of a "tertiary institution" is ____________________.
2. "Meals on wheels" is a program that ____________________
____________________.
3. "Extrovert" is a synonym to ____________________.
4. "To swap courses" means ____________________.

# Text Two

## I. Words and expressions

technical /ˈteknɪkəl/ *adj.* 技术的
questionnaire /ˌkwestʃəˈneə/ *n.* 调查问卷
dietary /ˈdaɪətərɪ/ *adj.* 饮食的
consultation /ˌkɒnsəlˈteɪʃən/ *n.* 咨询

## II. Listen to confirm or to adjust

*Listen and find out if your expectations are the same as or different from what you hear. If different, find the correct one or ones from **Make your prediction**.*

## III. Listen and answer the following questions.

1. What does it mean by "the colloquial language of Australians"?
____________________
____________________
2. What does it mean by "metabolic rate"?
____________________
____________________

## IV. Listen and fill in the following blanks with the missing information.

1. Anna's way of increasing her vocabulary:

a. Listening to ________________________________________.

b. Keeping a journal of ____________________________________.

2. Anna's involvement in a study project:

a. Subjects: a group of ________kids.

b. Method: questionnaire.

c. Findings: two major dietary problems with Australian kids were that many either ____________________________________________ or they ____________________________________________.

3. Anna's plan for the future:

a. Short-term: continue to work for ________________ and gain ________________.

b. Mid-term: get a position in a ____________________.

c. Long-term: open her ____________________ providing ____________________and giving ________________; or go back to __________________ and try to improve ________________________________________.

## Part Three Look at This

### 从上下文理解生词的意思

听力理解中的一个普遍问题是生词的障碍。其实我们捕捉生词词意的方法很多，比如可以通过上下文推测，可以借助词缀知识猜测，也可以在原文中寻找。人们在讲话时会有以下几种情况：

1. 有时说话人提到一个术语，随即考虑到听众的需要，给出相应的解释。如本单元中Anna具有营养学专业背景，提到metabolic rate之后，马上解释说the rate at which the body burns up food，这样听众就不难猜出metabolic rate的意思是新陈代谢的速度。

2. 有时说话人提到一个相对生僻的词，会给出一个同义词，如Anna讲到extrovert时，随即说出outgoing，同样为听众解决了生词的问题。

3. 有时说话人话中生词的意思可以在前文中找到，如Anna讲自己开始学广告，后来成绩不好。提到changed my direction，有心的听众就会猜到是指“换专业”。Anna意识到自己的性格不适合这门学科，转而进修营养学。当她讲完这段，采访人说了句So you swapped courses，如果听懂了Anna前面说的话，我们就能推断出swapped courses在这里就是转专业的意思。所以碰到生词，不妨前后联系起来听，这样就有可能扫除生词带来的障碍。

下面提供更多练习来操练在原文中捕捉生词词意的技巧。

# Part Four

## Here's More

### Exercise One

*Listen to the dialogues and answer the following questions.*

1. What does it mean by "amenities"?

______________________________________________

2. What does it mean by "I-20"?

______________________________________________

3. What does "ESL" stand for?

______________________________________________

4. Where can we find a book "on reserve"?

______________________________________________

### Exercise Two

*Listen to the monologues and choose the appropriate equivalent in Chinese for each of the following expressions.*

1. endoscope
   a. B 超
   b. 内窥镜

2. physiological shock
   a. 中风
   b. 电击

3. PTSD
   a. 记忆缺失
   b. 创伤后遗症

4. diversified portfolio
   a. 分散风险组合
   b. 分类目录

# Unit 12

# Working on Board the Plane

## Part One Before You Listen

### I. Think and answer

1. What is an ideal job in your opinion? In what way is it desirable?
2. What are the main responsibilities as far as the ideal job is concerned?
3. What qualifications should you have to get your desired job?
4. Is a high salary the only thing that counts while seeking employment? Why or why not?
5. How will you deal with the inconveniences brought about by your job in the future?

### II. Make your prediction

*Browse through all the information offered in this unit and predict the main idea of Text One and Text Two by choosing from a, b, c and d. You may choose more than one answer to indicate your prediction.*

**Text One**

a. Complaints of a flight attendant.
b. Feelings towards working as a flight attendant.
c. Main responsibility of a flight attendant.
d. Qualifications for being a flight attendant.

**Text Two**

a. Bad sides of being a flight attendant.

b. Changes in the type of services offered by the airline.
c. Satisfaction obtained from work.
d. Advice on choosing in-flight service as a career.

## Part Two Listen Now

### Text One

#### I. Words and expressions

exotic /ɪɡ'zɒtɪk/ *adj.* 奇异的；异国风情的
hospitality /ˌhɒspɪ'tæləti/ *n.* 殷勤；好客；食宿招待
cabin /'kæbɪn/ *n.* 客舱
preliminary /prɪ'lɪmɪnərɪ/ *adj.* 初步的；预备的
glamorous /'ɡlæmərəs/ *adj.* 富有魅力的；迷人的
roster /'rɒstə/ *n.* 值勤表，勤务表
long haul 长时间；远距离
TAFE (the Technical and Further Education College)（澳洲）专科技术学院

#### II. Listen to confirm or to adjust

*Listen and find out if your expectations are the same as or different from what you hear. If different, find the correct one or ones from **Make your prediction**.*

#### III. Listen and choose the best answer to each question you hear.

1. a. Only one year.
   b. Two years.
   c. About six years.
   d. About five years.

2. a. She received training in high school.
   b. She took a TAFE Associate Diploma.
   c. She received training from Australia Airways.
   d. She first took a TAFE Associate Diploma and then received training from Australia Airways.
3. a. She will stay at the best hotel rooms.
   b. She will meet new people.
   c. She will soon be off somewhere she hasn't been before.
   d. She never knows where she may be going.

## IV. Listen and decide whether the following statements are true (T) or false (F).

1. This interview is focused on the airline hospitality industry. *T* ☐ *F* ☐
2. Julie Nevard works for Australia Airways and is a junior member of the cabin crew staff. *T* ☐ *F* ☐
3. Flight attendants, according to Julie, are responsible for the needs and demands of each passenger as well as the safety of the plane and all the passengers. *T* ☐ *F* ☐
4. Julie's preliminary training at TAFE is her major professional qualification because it's more specialized. *T* ☐ *F* ☐

# Text Two

## I. Words and expressions

blockbuster /ˈblɒkˌbʌstə/ *n.* 轰动一时的东西(尤指风靡一时的电影、书籍)
upgrade /ʌpˈɡreɪd/ *v.* 给……升级；提升
carrier /ˈkærɪə/ *n.* 航空公司
vie /vaɪ/ *v.* (与某人)竞争(做某事)
gourmet /ˈɡʊəmeɪ/ *n.* 美食家，讲究饮食的人
commonplace /ˈkɒmənpleɪs/ *adj.* 普通的，一般的，常见的
galley /ˈɡælɪ/ *n.* 飞机上的厨房
ingredient /ɪnˈɡriːdjənt/ *n.* (混合物的)成分；(尤指烹饪中的)配料
time zone 时区
jet lag 飞行时差综合征

## II. Listen to confirm or to adjust

*Listen and find out if your expectations are the same as or different from what you hear. If different, find the correct one or ones from **Make your prediction**.*

## III. Listen and choose the best answer to each question you hear.

1. a. Hong Kong. b. New York.
   c. Bali. d. London.

2. a. 4. b. 3.
   c. 2. d. 1.

3. a. More critical passengers.
   b. Constant changing of time zones.
   c. Tougher competition among carriers.
   d. Attraction of the comfortable train ride.

## IV. Listen and fill in the following blanks with the missing information.

1. Julie deals with jet lag by ______________________________.
2. The two biggest improvements in in-flight services are ________________ and ________________.
3. Restriction on smoking has brought about two benefits: ________________ and ________________.
4. Julie considers her career to be __________ and __________, but __________, not as __________ as people usually think of it.

## Part Three Look at This

**抓住只言片语判断讲话人的职业**

在日常生活中往往有这样的情况：我们并不需要完整的信息，只需抓住只言片语就能判断讲话人在说些什么。在听母语中文时，这是我们驾轻就熟的事情，但在听英语时则需要不断训练才能达到这一步。这一单元着重讲如何抓住只言片语判断讲话人的职业。比如当我们单独听到下面这段取自本单元的录音时，可以利用常识和下面这段文字中的关键词（划线部分）来判断讲话人的职业。

**Julie:** That's hard to say really. Well, we're responsible for all the needs and demands of each and every passenger, for up to 10 hours on some long haul flights. Not to mention the safety of the plane and all the passengers. I suppose, if I have to come up with a single answer, it'd be passenger comfort.

抓住了划线部分的内容和由这些内容组成的句子的意思，加上常识，即便讲话者没有直接说出她的职业，我们也能毫不费力地知道她是空中乘务员。

下面再来归纳一下抓住只言片语判断讲话人职业时要注意的事项：

1. 集中精力抓住听力材料中的关键词或词组，如从事某项职业所需要的专业技能或个人品质，这些都有利于我们根据听到的描述作出正确的判断。

2. 掌握职业方面的常用词汇。下面对一些常见的与职业有关的词汇作一归纳：

professor（教授）; lecturer（讲师）; librarian（图书管理员）; secretary（秘书）; engineer（工程师）; mechanic（机修工）; electrician（电工）; plumber（管子工）; carpenter（木工）; merchant（商人）; cook（厨师）; tailor（裁缝）; dentist（牙医）; surgeon（外科医生）; plastic surgeon（整形外科医生）; physician（内科医生）; pharmacist（药剂师）; salesman（推销员）; real estate agent（房产中介）; cashier（出纳）; waitress（女服务员）; operator（电话接线员）; receptionist（前台接待）; novelist（小说家）; lawyer/solicitor/barrister（律师）; judge（法官）; florist（花商）; hairdresser/barber（理发师）; journalist（新闻工作者）; reporter（记者）; chauffeur（汽车司机）; conductor（售票员）; referee（裁判）; magician（魔术师）; attendant （服务员）; pilot（飞行员）; captain（船长）; diplomat（外交官）; ambassador（大使）; councilor（顾问）; supervisor（管理人，主管人）; general（将军）; statesman（政治家）; director（处长，局长，主任，董事）

## Part Four Here's More

### Exercise One

*Listen to the following ten short conversations carefully and choose the best answer to each question you hear.*

1. a. A writer.
   b. A teacher.

c. A reporter.
d. A student.

2. a. A math teacher and his colleague.
b. A teacher and his student.
c. A student and his classmate.
d. A librarian and a student.

3. a. A plumber.
b. An electrician.
c. A mechanic.
d. A repairman.

4. a. A doctor.
b. A nurse.
c. A bank clerk.
d. A cashier in the hospital.

5. a. She sells stoves and refrigerators.
b. She's an apartment manager.
c. She's a real estate agent.
d. She's a maid.

6. a. Doctor and patient.
b. Husband and wife.
c. Doctor and patient's family member.
d. Teacher and student.

7. a. A doctor.
b. The man's wife.
c. The man's sister.
d. The man's friend.

8. a. Plumber.
b. Laundry worker.
c. Carpenter.
d. Train conductor.

9. a. Florist.
b. Dentist.
c. Organist.
d. Pharmacist.

10. a. Cook.
b. Cashier.

c. Waitress.
d. Manager.

## Exercise Two

*Listen twice to the five people talking about their jobs and complete the following table.*

| | Jobs | Professional skills | Personal qualities |
|---|---|---|---|
| The 1st speaker | 1. ________ | 2. ________ | 3. ________ |
| The 2nd speaker | 4. ________ | 5. ________ | 6. ________ |
| The 3rd speaker | 7. ________ | 8. ________ | 9. ________ |
| The 4th speaker | 10. ________ | 11. ________ | 12. ________ |
| The 5th speaker | 13. ________ | 14. ________ | 15. ________ |

# Unit 13

# Achieving Career Success

## Part One Before You Listen

### I. Think and answer

1. How do you define success?
2. What qualities are indispensable to achieving success in one's career?
3. How will you prepare yourself to achieve success in your future career?
4. Do you know your own SWOTs, that is, strengths, weaknesses, opportunities and threats?
5. What will you do to make your college life a success?

### II. Make your prediction

*Browse through all the information offered in this unit and predict the main idea of Text One and Text Two by choosing from a, b, c and d. You may choose more than one answer to indicate your prediction.*

**Text One**

a. Advice on working for oneself.
b. Inspirational stories of successful people.
c. Qualities leading to success.
d. Differences in starting styles.

**Text Two**

a. Pleasure of working for oneself.
b. Preparation for working for oneself.

c. Personal experience in working for oneself.

d. Problems with working for oneself.

## Part Two Listen Now

### Text One

#### I. Words and expressions

rector /ˈrektə/ *n.* 学院院长，学校校长
retail /ˈriːteɪl/ *n.* 零售，零卖
inventory /ˈɪnvəntərɪ/ *n.* 存货清单；库存
biography /baɪˈɒgrəfɪ/ *n.* 传记
motivational /ˌməʊtɪˈveɪʃənəl/ *adj.* 有动力的；提供动力的
notch /nɒtʃ/ *n.* 等，级

#### II. Listen to confirm or to adjust

*Listen and find out if your expectations are the same as or different from what you hear. If different, find the correct one or ones from **Make your prediction**.*

#### III. Listen and choose the best answer to each question you hear.

1. a. Because business is a game he plays to win.
   b. Because he values freedom and choices that success brings.
   c. Because he takes a lot of effort pleasing co-workers.
   d. Because he is confident of his abilities.

2. a. They can get promotions quickly.
   b. They can get the chance to enter management.
   c. They can get experience and knowledge.
   d. They can derive a lot of pleasure from their work.

3. a. Get face to face with clients.
   b. Get face to face with himself.
   c. Read inspirational books.
   d. Listen to some music.

## IV. Listen and answer the following questions.

1. According to Ross, what kind of job should a person get if he is not confident of his abilities to work for himself?

   ______________________________

2. What does Ross do to keep learning and challenging himself?

   ______________________________

3. Why did Henry Ford keep asking his engineers about that V8 engine?

   ______________________________

4. What did Henry Ford think his job was?

   ______________________________

# Text Two

## I. Words and expressions

goody /ˈgʊdɪ/ *n.* 可口的食物
hum /hʌm/ *v.* 发出嗡嗡声
paycheck /ˈpeɪtʃek/ *n.* 工资
dribble /ˈdrɪbl/ *n.* 细流；少量
trait /treɪt/ *n.* 特性；品质；性格

## II. Listen to confirm or to adjust

*Listen and find out if your expectations are the same as or different from what you hear. If different, find the correct one or ones from **Make your prediction**.*

## III. Listen and decide whether the following statements are true (T) or false (F).

1. Ross was the only one left among the ten who went out on   *T* ☐   *F* ☐

their own because he was the most qualified.

2. It was fortunate of Ross to get his wife's understanding. *T* ☐ *F* ☐

3. Ross had always had the habit of waking up early and getting some work done in the morning. *T* ☐ *F* ☐

4. You can drop by your client or call for arrangement according to Ross. *T* ☐ *F* ☐

## IV. Listen and fill in the following blanks with the missing information.

1. Ross tried to be most effective by ________________.
2. Ross found it no longer difficult for him to get out of bed in the morning because ________________.
3. Other than the lazy, or those without the freedom to dedicate themselves to the task, there are ________________ that might disqualify someone from working for themselves.
4. In Ross's opinion, selling is easy because you ________________ ________ and then you ________________.

# Part Three Look at This

### 从上下文理解短语的意思

短语在听力中是最棘手的一部分。短语都由简单而常用的词汇组成，但这些熟悉的词经过固定的组合之后，往往让你不知所云，例如be on the ball（勤奋地从事某事），be in the air（没有确定，悬而未决；到处传播）。短语一般可以分为两类：一类是固定的动词词组（two-or-three-word verbal phrases），例如stay up（熬夜），call off（取消），bring up（抚养）等；另外一类是习语（idiomatic expressions），例如beat around the bush（拐弯抹角），do something with flying colors（很出色地完成任务）。在这一单元的访谈中两种类型的短语都出现了。例如当谈到阅读名人传记时，采访者问：Is there one biography you have read that stands out?这里stand out 就是一个动词词组，而Ross 在回答时提到了Henry Ford 的传记给他留下了深刻的印象，根据上下文我们可以推测出stand out是“最杰出，最出色”的意思。又比如在第二段对话中，Ross 提到my wife and I are on the same page，如果我们注意到lucky 和后面的she understands, 就不难推测出 be on the same page 是“互相理解”的意思。两段对话中还有 get off their butts，beat the bush 等短语，留心上下文，意思都很容易推测出。这两类短语的共同特点是我们很难从字面理解其意思，所以当我们听到短语时，不妨试着从上下文来推测其意义，抓住关键词语和细节来推断。当然我们平时还需要多听、多读，不断地积累，从而更好地理解短语。

## Here's More

### Exercise One

*Listen to the following statements carefully and choose from a, b, c and d the one which is the closest in meaning to each statement you hear.*

1. a. Michael can throw stones at the library from his house.
   b. Michael lives close to the library.
   c. Michael's house has stones thrown on it.
   d. There's a stone path from Michael's house to the library.

2. a. Kate has already disposed of the chemicals.
   b. Kate didn't do the last assignment in chemistry.
   c. Kate was unhappy about the newest assignment.
   d. Kate was excited about the chemistry assignment.

3. a. Margaret's headache kept her out of class.
   b. Margaret is by far the best writer in her class.
   c. Margaret finds writing a restful activity.
   d. Margaret is taller than all the others at school.

4. a. Mary asked the teacher a question.
   b. Mary's question was off the subject.
   c. Mary's idea was reasonable.
   d. Mary's idea was impossible.

5. a. He has part-time work in the laboratory.
   b. He likes the experimental aspects of his work.
   c. He has done all the laboratory experiments already.
   d. He asked for the day off from work today.

6. a. It was Lita who wanted to make an appointment.
   b. It will take Lita a long time to visit California.
   c. Lita saw some shells near the sea.
   d. Lita will visit San Francisco.

7. a. Not many people enjoy that kind of music.
   b. It took a while for that music to become popular.
   c. The public's first reaction to that music was positive.
   d. You'd never catch me listening to that kind of music.

8. a. Bill was given a speeding ticket by the patrolman.
   b. Bill was speeding when he saw the patrolman.
   c. Bill was about to speed when he saw the policeman.
   d. Bill told the policeman that he had not been speeding.

9. a. The family had just enough money to buy groceries.
   b. The family was unable to manage their money.
   c. The family bought nothing due to the high prices.
   d. The family earned sixty dollars by managing the grocery.

10. a. Your advisor put a sign up on the door.
    b. Your advisor is quite tall.
    c. You may have to get glasses after all.
    d. You should talk to your advisor before entering your name.

## Exercise Two

*Listen to the following ten short conversations carefully and choose the best answer to each question you hear.*

1. a. She wants to get back to work in the morning.
   b. She is happy to stop working.
   c. She will call him in the evening.
   d. She thinks they should go on after a break.

2. a. She needs some help rolling the ball.
   b. She needs some help with her game.
   c. She thinks it is a good idea to get started.
   d. She doesn't care what sports they play.

3. a. His teeth hurt him very much.
   b. He decided to take the course next semester instead.
   c. He has no time for meals.
   d. He finds the work harder than he expected.

4. a. The woman blames the man for his absence.
   b. The woman thinks that everything was all right.
   c. The woman thanks the man for his efforts.
   d. The woman doesn't think it was the man's fault.

5. a. The woman is watching an exciting film with the man.
   b. The woman can't be photographed with the lake in the background.
   c. The woman is running toward the lake.
   d. The woman is filming the lake.

6. a. Wendy's choice of subject.
   b. Wendy's condescending attitude.
   c. Wendy's negligence.
   d. Wendy's irrelevant response.

7. a. She can't send the message right now.
   b. She has to post a letter instead.
   c. She has to turn down the man's request.
   d. She's not sure if the computer is fixed.

8. a. The bread should be given to the horses.
   b. It will taste better if it is heated.
   c. They need to wait a little while.
   d. The man needs to keep calm.

9. a. She doesn't want to make the speech.
   b. She doesn't want to give Karen money for the shoes.
   c. She would prefer that the man give her the present.
   d. She needs to give back her shoes.

10. a. To run into each other.
    b. To get bargains.
    c. To avoid the crowds.
    d. To join the crowds.

# Unit 14

# Farming

## Part One Before You Listen

### I. Think and answer

1. What do you think the supply and demand market is?
2. Have you ever thought of living in a rural area? And why?
3. What advantages do you think children who grow up on a farm or a ranch have over those who grow up in a city?

### II. Make your prediction

*Browse through all the information offered in this unit and predict the main idea of Text One and Text Two by choosing from a, b, c and d. You may choose more than one answer to indicate your prediction.*

**Text One**

a. Raising cattle is the main activity of American farmers.
b. Cattle business in the US is not necessarily profitable.
c. People choose to be farmers or ranchers because they like the job.
d. Many farmers don't like office work because it is too boring.

**Text Two**

a. A farmer's wife usually cooks meals, cleans the house and looks after the kids.
b. Sharon talks about the possible financial problems in operating a farm or a ranch.
c. Sharon talks about her life as a rancher's wife.
d. There are both advantages and disadvantages for children to grow up on the farm.

## Part Two

## Listen Now

### Text One

#### I. Words and expressions

profitable /ˈprɒfɪtəbl/ *adj.* 有赢利的；有利可图的
fluctuate /ˈflʌktjʊeɪt/ *v.* 波动；起伏
breed /briːd/ *v.* 生育；繁殖 *n.* 种类
calf /kɑːf/ *n.* 小牛
ranch /rɑːntʃ;ræntʃ/ *n.* 大牧场；大农场
rancher /ˈrɑːntʃə; ˈræntʃə/ *n.* 大牧场(农场)主
livestock /ˈlaɪvstɒk/ *n.* (总称)家畜，牲畜
raiser /ˈreɪzə/ *n.* 饲养者
bring on 引起；导致；使发生
tie up 使(资金等)搁死而不能随便挪用
in terms of 在……方面，从……方面说来

#### II. Listen to confirm or to adjust

*Listen and find out if your expectations are the same as or different from what you hear. If different, find the correct one or ones from* ***Make your prediction****.*

#### III. Listen and choose the best answer to each question you hear.

1. a. Cattle business.
   b. Cow business.
   c. Calf business.
   d. Beef business.

2. a. Only one year.
   b. No more than one year.
   c. Around one and a half years.
   d. No less than one year and a half.

3. a. They feel isolated.
   b. They feel bored.
   c. Both *a* and *b*.
   d. Neither *a* nor *b*.

4. a. Go to a restaurant.
   b. Go to a movie.
   c. Drive through the cows and check them.
   d. Sell the cows and buy new and young ones.

5. a. It's hard but very interesting.
   b. It is hard and dull.
   c. It is not difficult at all.
   d. It is more interesting than that of people living in the city.

## IV. Listen and fill in the following blanks with the missing information.

1. Cattle raising is not always __________ because the price of cattle __________ with the market and sometimes it is below ______________. In addition, cattle raisers usually have no idea about what next year will ___________ the market and have to _______________ continually for a certain length of time before getting marketable calves. Therefore some people consider cattle raising a/an ___________ business and wonder why people want to be farmers or ranchers.
2. It is true that farmers in the rural area do not have so many __________ for recreation and _____________ as people in the city. However, for a farmer who ________ his way of life, living and working in the city is more likely to _______ him.

# Text Two

## I. Words and expressions

equity /ˈekwɪtɪ/ *n.* (无固定利息的)股票
outweigh /ˌaʊtˈweɪ/ *v.* 超过
self-reliant /ˌselfrɪˈlaɪənt/ *adj.* 自力更生的

## II. Listen to confirm or to adjust

*Listen and find out if your expectations are the same as or different from what you hear. If different, find the correct one or ones from* ***Make your prediction****.*

## III. Listen and choose the best answer to complete each of the following sentences.

1. Ranchers can feel very insecure especially if ________.
   a. they have one or two bad years
   b. their beef is not good enough
   c. the price of beef fluctuates
   d. None of the above.

2. According to Sharon, ranchers can ________ to avoid financial disaster.
   a. borrow money from the bank
   b. sell their ranch
   c. sell the equity in their ranch
   d. pay off their ranch

3. Unlike most suburban housewives, Sharon can't have much free time because ________.
   a. she has more children to take care of
   b. she has to get out and work with her husband
   c. she has far more housework to do
   d. her husband wants her to work in the same way as he does

4. We can infer that ________.
   a. there is no difference between ranch life and city life
   b. children living in the rural area can always be with their parents and learn to work
   c. Sharon couldn't spend a lot of time with her children even when they were small
   d. most working mothers in the city can't be with their children when they are at work

5. The way children grow up on a farm helps them ________.
   a. become independent
   b. learn to work
   c. learn responsibility
   d. All of the above.

## IV. Listen and decide whether the following statements are true (T) or false (F).

| | | |
|---|---|---|
| 1. It is mentioned in this interview that if a woman doesn't like farming or ranching, she wouldn't marry a farmer or a rancher. | *T* ☐ | *F* ☐ |
| 2. There are still some women in the rural area who live a life just like suburban housewives. | *T* ☐ | *F* ☐ |
| 3. The problem of financial security doesn't bother Sharon too much and instead, she considers it something to live with or a fact of life. | *T* ☐ | *F* ☐ |
| 4. Sharon is not so busy as a working mother in the city. | *T* ☐ | *F* ☐ |

5. In spite of some advantages, there are more disadvantages for children growing up in the rural area.

## Part Three Look at This

### 抓住重复内容，找出实质性的信息

采访是两人之间或者更多人之间的信息交流和思想沟通。通常，采访人或被采访人会有意无意地重复对方说过的话或其中的某些词语，以确保双方的交流和沟通得以顺利进行。有时，一方重复另一方的话是为了核实自己对对方所表达的意思理解无误；有时则是为了强调同意(或不同意)对方的看法。那么怎样来判断被重复部分所传递的信息呢？首先要联系上下文来听，其次要关注被重复部分的语气和语调。请看本单元采访中的实例：

1. **Interviewer:** It must be a very profitable business then …

   **Bob Becker:** Uh … not necessarily.

   **Interviewer:** It's not necessarily a … a profitable business?

2. **Interviewer:** So the price is fluctuating all the time …

   **Bob Becker:** Right. It fluctuates, and it can get below production costs.

3. **Bob Becker:** They cook the meals, and they clean the house and that's it — take care of the kids …

   **Interviewer:** Have you known … have you known some situations like that?

   **Bob Becker:** Oh, yeah, I know situations like that!

例1中，采访人重复Bob的话是表示惊讶，养牛并不一定会赢利出乎采访人的意料。在重复时，采访人用的应该是升调。

例2中，Bob为了肯定采访人的结论而重复了关键词fluctuate(应该用降调重复)。双方共同传递着一个信息，即价格一直在起伏。被采访人进而补充说价格有时甚至低于成本。其实他在这里也道出了养牛为什么不一定赢利的原因。

例3中，Bob重复situations like that是为了确保双方谈论的是同一话题，即，生活在乡村的家庭主妇们的生活状况。

然而我们要注意的是，说话者并不一定总是重复同样的词语，有时他们也会使用一些近义词或意思上相互承接、紧密联系的词语。例如在本单元中我们曾听到：

1. **Bob Becker:** You've got a year, to a year and a half, tied up there …

   **Interviewer:** So, you're making an investment all the time …

   **Bob Becker:** Right. So you're not sure.

2. **Interviewer:** So … it's not something that bothers you terribly. I mean, that

… you … it's a fact of life. It's sort of …

**Sharon Becker:** Something you live with, yeah …

在例 1 中，tied up 和 make an investment all the time 意思上紧密联系，都是在说资金在从(养牛)投入到产出这段时间内不仅无法随意挪动，而且需要不断的注入。

在例 2 中，a fact of life 和 something you live with 意思上是相近的，对话双方表达的是同一个意思。

## Part Four Here's More

### Exercise

*You will hear several short dialogues with repetition. Listen carefully and fill in the following blanks with the missing information. (One word for each blank.)*

1. John has a feeling of ______________ although he is ______________ ________________. So he has to work hard to avoid being sent down someday.
2. Most ranchers and farmers don't want to organize ____________ __________________ because the price of their products doesn't warrant union-paid-scale labor.
3. Thanks to the Daniel Boone __________________, which has been broadcast on TV around the world, Mckennon becomes known to people in many countries.
4. It is ____________________ ____________________ that policewomen don't do the same thing as men do.
5. Surely, there is ____________________ ____________________ between working for oneself and for a big company. For example, you may be more conscious of time when working for a big company.
6. In a big company, it is very common that only a few employees know the top management and almost none of them see their boss. Therefore, many people think a big company is quite ________________.
7. When asked about _______________ _____________ _________________ _______________ she has had to deal with, Sara says she has seen things that she is supposed to see only once in a lifetime.
8. It is said that a lady bought a ____________________ ____________________ for her dog and slept on the floor with the dog for ____________________ ____________________.

# Unit 15

# People Skills

## Part One Before You Listen

### I. Think and answer

1. How do you get along with people around you?
2. Do you think a competent person can always achieve success in his/her work? And why?
3. In your opinion, do people need to learn some skills in communicating with others? And what people skills do you know?

### II. Make your prediction

*Browse through all the information offered in this unit and predict the main idea of Text One and Text Two by choosing from a, b, c and d. You may choose more than one answer to indicate your prediction.*

**Text One**

a. Debra has published a book called *Lions Don't Need to Roar.*
b. People are born with something for success.
c. According to Debra, relearning people skills is important and can help people become successful in their work.
d. Try to look confident, which is a people skill.

**Text Two**

a. Usually people do business on a handshake basis.
b. It is so easy to forget the name of the person whom you are just introduced to.

c. Debra introduces some skills to help people remember others' names when they meet for the first time.

d. Debra introduces more skills to help people get others' names again when they forget them.

## Part Two Listen Now

### Text One

#### I. Words and expressions

major /ˈmeɪdʒə/ *v.* 主修
economics /ˌiːkəˈnɒmɪks/ *n.* 经济学
formula /ˈfɔːmjʊlə/ *n.* 方案；配方；处方
unlearn /ˌʌnˈlɜːn/ *v.* 忘记；抛掉
socialize /ˈsəʊʃəlaɪz/ *v.* 使适应社会需要；使适合过社会生活
professional /prəʊˈfeʃənəl/ *adj.* 职业的；从事特定专业的
constipate /ˈkɒnstɪpeɪt/ *v.* 使迟钝；使呆滞
consultant /kənˈsʌltənt/ *n.* 咨询专家；顾问
dynamic /daɪˈnæmɪk/ *adj.* 有生气的
project /prəʊˈdʒekt/ *v.* 表现出
verbally /ˈvɜːbəlɪ/ *adv.* 口头地，非书面地
approach /əˈprəʊtʃ/ *v.* 靠近，接近
dawdle /ˈdɔːdl/ *v.* 浪费(时间)
expense account 费用账户
figure out 想出
split second 一刹那

#### II. Listen to confirm or to adjust

*Listen and find out if your expectations are the same as or different from what you hear. If different, find the correct one or ones from* ***Make your prediction****.*

## III. Listen and choose the best answer to each question you hear.

1. a. Sales.
   b. Public relation.
   c. Economics and finance.
   d. Economics.

2. a. Because we are not born with it.
   b. Because we lose it as we enter the society.
   c. Because we always try to move up.
   d. Because we don't get enough education.

3. a. He leaves a bad taste in your mouth.
   b. There's just poor chemistry between you.
   c. He's quite dynamic and fits in well.
   d. He's not dynamic enough.

4. a. Some competent people are fired probably because they don't know how to show their competence.
   b. Tricks can become habits.
   c. It is impossible for people to keep genuine after they relearn people skills.
   d. None of the above.

## IV. Listen and fill in the following blanks with the missing information.

1. According to Debra, we are born with the skills for success but we unlearn them when we get __________ and __________. In a word, what we had when we were young is what we ______________________ now but we have lost.
2. Debra was ________________ when she knew that she was fired because she ________ people skills. But fortunately she took advantage of the ______ and finally became a ________ and even published a book about how to relearn people skills.
3. As an interviewee, first, you should ________ slightly after walking into the room. In this way you non-verbally __________________ your presence and give the interviewer some time to __________________ his or her work at hand and give you the ______________ _______. Then when you ______________ him or her, don't hurry like you're anxious. You can shake hands and ______________ a split second longer.

## Text Two

### I. Words and expressions

basis /ˈbeɪsɪs/ *n.* 基础
figuratively /ˈfɪgjʊrətɪvlɪ/ *adv.* 象征地
tone /təʊn/ *n.* 气氛
gathering /ˈgæðərɪŋ/ *n.* 集会；聚集
self-conscious /ˌselfˈkɒnʃəs/ *adj.* 不自然的，忸怩的
self-aware /ˌselfəˈweə/ *adj.* 自我意识的；自知的
thereafter /ˌðeərˈɑːftə/ *adv.* 此后，以后
shameful /ˈʃeɪmfʊl/ *adj.* 可耻的；丢脸的
block /blɒk/ *v.* 阻碍；阻挡

### II. Listen to confirm or to adjust

*Listen and find out if your expectations are the same as or different from what you hear. If different, find the correct one or ones from **Make your prediction**.*

### III. Listen and choose the best answers to complete each of the following sentences. (More than one answer to each question.)

1. Handshake is very important because ________.
   a. it is the first time people get to touch
   b. it enables people to hear each other's name
   c. it sets the whole tone
   d. it helps businessmen a lot

2. We sometimes miss other people's names probably because ________.
   a. we are self-conscious and self-aware when we are introduced to them
   b. we are not intelligent enough
   c. we just listen to ensure that our names are pronounced correctly
   d. we do not hear their names clearly

3. In order to remember the other person's name when we meet for the first time, we can ________.
   a. write it down
   b. slow down and listen for it

c. ask him or her to repeat again and again

d. use it in the conversation after hearing it

## IV. Listen and fill in the following blanks with the missing information.

*There are many ways to get the other person's name again. For example:*

1. You can say, " ________________________________";
2. You can ________ your hand and give your name first;
3. With an ____________________________ attitude, you can say, "You know, we met, and ________________________________________________ the other night. I can't remember everyone's name, I'm sorry, uh …" to invite him or her to give his or her name once again;
4. You can say, "Your face is so familiar, and my — I've just ________________________" when you are confronted with such a question as "Hi, you remember me, don't you?"

## Part Three Look at This

### 多听多练，培养对音变的敏感度

在连贯的讲话中，一些单词的读音会发生变化，如果我们在听的过程中缺乏对音变现象的敏感度，那么听力理解或多或少会受到影响。连贯的讲话中读音的变化大致有以下几类：

1）连读，即前一个音节或词末尾的辅音和下一个音节或词开首的元音连读。例如：Are you born <u>with it</u> /wɪðɪt/?，<u>As I</u> /æzaɪ/ say, …。

2）弱读。一般句子中次要的单词（比如助动词、冠词、介词、连词及代词）的元音可以弱读，如 ...pause ever <u>so</u> /sə/ slightly…。除了 /əʊ/，其他的音如 /æ/，/u:/，/aʊə/，/ɔ:ə/，/ɑ:ə/ 都可弱读为 /ə/。

3）省音，即省略某个音。一般如果前一个音节或单词的词尾是辅音，后一个音节或单词的词首也是辅音，那么前一个音节或单词词尾的辅音不发音。不发音的辅音有 /p/，/t/，/k/，/b/，/d/，/g/，/f/，/v/，例如 And a <u>lot that</u> /lɒðæt/ we had …。并且当 he，him，his，her，have 与前面的单词连读时，h 不发音。

4）同化，即一个音受相邻音的影响，趋向相邻音的发音或发第三个音。比如，以 /t/ 结尾的音节或单词遇上以元音开头的音节或单词，/t/ 发 /d/ 的音；而以 /t/，/d/，/s/，/z/ 结尾的音节或单词接以字母 y 开头的音节或单词，会产生第三个音。例如：… <u>put your</u> /pʊtʃə/ hand in your lap，… you can <u>extend your</u> /ɪkstendʒə/ hand and say …。

要想克服音变给听者带来的障碍，我们还需要在了解其规律的基础上配合一定的练习，多读（大声朗读）、多听（听原声资料，如英语歌曲等）、多写（听写），以便培养对音变现象的敏感度，成功地理解听力内容。

## Part Four Here's More

### Exercise One

*Listen to each sentence and underline the part where there is a change in pronunciation. Then listen again and read after the recording.*

1. She sat two rows in front of us. She had a bright yellow shirt on.
2. Would you mind my sitting here?
3. And I want to see if his band can play at my birthday party.
4. I've had enough. I don't know what to think of her anymore.
5. Mary looks so different now.
6. I heard that you just quit. I just can't believe it.
7. The waiter repeated, "Cash or charge?" But the foreign visitor still couldn't understand him.
8. I'm throwing out the food that made you sick at dinner the other night.
9. I got you the book you wanted. Here it is.
10. This test ranks your abilities.
11. She made those rolls you like. So why not come and have some?
12. He's trying to get hold of you.

### Exercise Two

*You will listen to a short conversation and a song with changes in pronunciation. Listen and fill in the following blanks.*

**A short conversation**

A: Your (1) ______________________________. Turkey sandwich for Mrs. Jones.

B: (2) ______________________________ meeting.

A: Tuna club for Betty.

B: (3) ______________________________ the phone.

A: (4) ______________________________?

B: That's mine. How much is it?

A: That'll be (5) ______________________________ bucks.

B: Here's five. Keep the change.

A: Thanks. (6) ______________________________, I'll just wait for the other ladies.

B: Sure, have a seat.

**A song: Country Roads**

Almost heaven
West Virginia
Blue Ridge Mountains
Shenandoah River
(7) ______________________________ there
Older than the trees
Younger than the mountains
Growing (8)______________________________

Country roads take me home
To the place I belong
West Virginia
Mountain Mama
(9) ________________________ country roads

All my memories
Gather round her
Miner's lady
Stranger to blue water
Dark and dusty
(10) ________________________ the sky
Misty taste of moonshine
(11) ________________________ my eyes

Country roads take me home
To the place I belong
West Virginia
Mountain Mama
Take me home country roads

I hear her (12) ________________________ the morning hours
She calls me
The radio reminds me of my home far away
And driving down the road
I (13) ________________________________
That I (14) ___________________________________
Yesterday, yesterday

Country roads take me home
To the place I belong
West Virginia
Mountain Mama
Take me home country roads

# Unit 16

# Magic Disney World

## Part One Before You Listen

### I. Think and answer

1. What do you know about Disneyland?
2. What do you think of Walt Disney?
3. What, in your opinion, are the crucial factors leading to success?
4. Who are the people you admire most? Why do you admire them?
5. How can you achieve success in your future career?

### II. Make your prediction

*Browse through all the information offered in this unit and predict the main idea of Text One and Text Two by choosing from a, b, c and d. You may choose more than one answer to indicate your prediction.*

**Text One**

a. Walt Disney's background.
b. Walt Disney's education.
c. The first appearance of Mickey Mouse.
d. Establishment of the Disney Studios.

**Text Two**

a. Crucial factors leading to Walt Disney's success.
b. Cartoon films produced by the Disney Studios.

c. Development of Disneyland.

d. Awards received by Walt Disney.

## Part Two Listen Now

### Text One

#### I. Words and expressions

experimental /ɪkˌsperɪ'mentəl/ *adj.* 实验的；试验性的
illustrator /'ɪləstreɪtə/ *n.* 插图画家
Kansas /'kænzəs/ City 堪萨斯城(美国密苏里州城市)
Missouri /mɪ'zʊərɪ/ 密苏里州(美国)

#### II. Listen to confirm or to adjust

*Listen and find out if your expectations are the same as or different from what you hear. If different, find the correct one or ones from **Make your prediction**.*

#### III. Listen and complete the following table.

| **Name** | Walt Disney, (1) ____________ of Mickey Mouse and (2) ___________ of Disneyland and (3) ______________. |
|---|---|
| **Time of birth** | (4) _______________ |
| **Place of birth** | (5) _______________ |
| **Experiences** | Worked as a driver for the (6) ___________ during (7) ___________;<br>Returned to (8) ______________, met Ub Iwerks and worked together on a series of (9) ____________________;<br>Set off to (10) ____________ and joined (11)_______;<br>Invented Mickey Mouse in (12) _________;<br>Gathered a team of (13) ______ and started to produce the famous cartoons. |

## IV. Listen and fill in the following blanks with the missing information.

1. Walt Disney first studied cartooning by doing a ____________________.
2. The first character that Walt Disney and Ub Iwerks invented was ____________________.
3. Mickey first appeared in the first ______________________ which was named *Steamboat Willie*.
4. Roy Disney was the ______________________ of Disney Studios and Walt was more the __________________________________.

# Text Two

## I. Words and expressions

apparently /əˈpærəntlɪ/ *adv.* 显然；据说
visualization /ˌvɪzjʊəlaɪˈzeɪʃən/ *n.* 设想，想象
feature /ˈfiːtʃə/ *n.* (电影的)正片，故事片
release /rɪˈliːs/ *v.* 使(新影片或唱片)上映或发行
censor /ˈsensə/ *n.* (书刊、电影等的)审查员，审查官
medium /ˈmiːdɪəm/ *n.* 传播媒介；艺术形式
prototype /ˈprəʊtəʊtaɪp/ *n.* 原型，雏型
presumably /prɪˈzjuːməblɪ/ *adv.* 可能，大概
vulgar /ˈvʌlgə/ *adj.* 粗俗的，庸俗的，低级的

## II. Listen to confirm or to adjust

*Listen and find out if your expectations are the same as or different from what you hear. If different, find the correct one or ones from* ***Make your prediction****.*

## III. Listen and choose the best answer to each question you hear.

1. a. In 1935.
   b. In 1940.
   c. In 1941.
   d. In 1964.

2. a. $16, 000,000.

b. $12,000,000.
c. $17,000,000.
d. $2,000,000.

3. a. 4.
b. 3.
c. 2.
d. 5.

## IV. Listen and decide whether the following statements are true (T) or false (F).

1. Walt could not only draw very well but also tell very amazing stories. *T* ☐ *F* ☐
2. The British film censor gave *Snow White and the Seven Dwarfs* an Adult certificate because it was very expensive. *T* ☐ *F* ☐
3. Disney started to produce films directly for television because he saw the potential of the medium. *T* ☐ *F* ☐
4. Walt never thought of opening the Disney World in Orlando, Florida when he was alive. *T* ☐ *F* ☐

# Look at This

### 百年迪斯尼

迪斯尼公司创建于1923年，当时仅仅是沃尔特·迪斯尼和罗伊·迪斯尼两兄弟的Disney Brothers Cartoon Studio，而现在它已经成为世界上第二大传媒公司，并在全球经营多家迪斯尼主题公园，每年收入达250亿美元。迪斯尼致力于为人们提供最特别的娱乐体验，并且一直秉承着对质量和创新不断追求的优良传统，而这一切都得益于公司创始人沃尔特·迪斯尼。

沃尔特·迪斯尼是美国动画片制作家、演出主持人和电影制片人，他制作了世界上第一部有声动画片《威利汽船》(1928年)和第一部动画长片《白雪公主》(1938年)。沃尔特·迪斯尼是一个传奇，他的名字就是一种梦想的象征。他于1928年创造了米老鼠这一经典卡通形象，被称为“米老鼠之父”。他还制作了电影史上第一部完整的动画影片，创建了迪斯尼主题公园，组建了现代化多媒体公司。沃尔特·迪斯尼的创意改变了世界的面貌，他是20世纪的英雄，而他谈及自己的事业时却说：“一切都是从一只老鼠开始的。”

## Part Four Here's More

### Exercise One

*You will hear a passage. Listen carefully and fill in the following blanks with the missing information.*

Hong Kong Disneyland is a (1) ________________ at Hong Kong Disneyland Resort. It was constructed by The Walt Disney Company and the (2) ________________ on reclaimed land from the Penny's Bay, Lantau Island, Hong Kong, China. The park was officially opened to visitors at 13:00 local time on Monday, (3) ________________; although VIPs and winners of a ticket lottery were allowed entry on a number of "test days" held before the grand opening. A (4) ________________ of Hong Kong Disneyland is the widely use of two languages, English and Chinese (both in Traditional and Simplified forms) in its (5) ________________. On (6) ________________, a special ceremony was held in the park to commemorate the placing of the tallest turret of (7) ________________. Present were Tung Chee Hwa, former Chief Executive of Hong Kong SAR; Jay Rasulo, President of Disney Parks and Resorts; Michael Eisner, CEO of the Walt Disney Company; and Mickey Mouse and other (8) ________________. Hong Kong Disneyland has the shortest (9) ________________ among all Disneylands, possibly because it is the smallest Disneyland.

The park features four themed lands similar to those at other Disney Parks: Main Street, USA; (10) ________________; Fantasyland; and (11) ________________. It will also feature a daily parade and (12) ________________.

### Exercise Two

*You will hear a passage. Listen carefully and answer the following questions.*

1. What did David Low, the late British political cartoonist, think of Walt Disney?

   ________________________________________

2. How many honors and citations did Walt Disney and his members of staff receive?

   ________________________________________

3. How many universities are mentioned in the passage from which Walt Disney received honorary degrees?

   ________________________________________

4. How many other personal awards are mentioned that Walt Disney received in his lifetime?

   ________________________________________

5. Of what descent were Walt Disney's father and mother?

   ________________________________________

# Unit 17 Global Warming

## Part One Before You Listen

### I. Think and answer

1. What do you think are the issues of the environment?
2. Do you live in a city or in the country? What do you think is the difference between the temperature, especially in summer, in a city and in the country?
3. Ask an elder if they think it's getting colder or warmer these years as compared to, say, twenty years ago.
4. Do you think our planet is going to get warmer or colder? What will be the consequence either way?

### II. Make your prediction

*Browse through all the information offered in this unit and predict the main idea of Text One and Text Two by choosing from a, b, c and d. You may choose more than one answer to indicate your prediction.*

**Text One**

a. White pollution.
b. Housing shortage.
c. Global warming.
d. Hurricanes.

### Text Two

a. Ways to improve the environment.

b. Ways to measure the ocean temperature.

c. Ways to predict disastrous weather.

d. Ways to prevent pollution.

## Part Two Listen Now

### Text One

#### I. Words and expressions

fizzle /ˈfɪzl/ *v.* 衰退
insulator /ˈɪnsjʊleɪtə/ *n.* 隔离物
radiate /ˈreɪdɪeɪt/ *v.* 辐射
insulation /ˌɪnsjʊˈleɪʃən/ *n.* 隔离
verify /ˈverɪfaɪ/ *v.* 证明
surge /sɜːdʒ/ *v.* 上升
subside /səbˈsaɪd/ *v.* 下降
fluctuation /ˌflʌktjʊˈeɪʃən/ *n.* 波动
reservoir /ˈrezəvwɑː/ *n.* 储备

#### II. Listen to confirm or to adjust

*Listen and find out if your expectations are the same as or different from what you hear. If different, find the correct one or ones from **Make your prediction**.*

#### III. Listen carefully and decide whether the interviewee, Dr. Clarke, agrees with the following statements. Write T (true) if you think he agrees, and F (false) if you think he doesn't.

1. Global warming is no longer a threat to human beings. *T* ☐ *F* ☐

2. Green house effect is a natural phenomenon. *T* ☐ *F* ☐

3. The earth may get warmer because of the green house effect. *T* ☐ *F* ☐

4. Temperature will increase by about a third of a degree every ten years. *T* ☐ *F* ☐

5. It is difficult to make prediction of the temperature change because the earth's temperature surges and subsides naturally. *T* ☐ *F* ☐

6. The best way of detecting global temperature change is to measure the temperature of the oceans as accurately as possible. *T* ☐ *F* ☐

## IV. Listen to some parts of the interview and answer the following questions by choosing the right answer from the two choices marked *a* and *b*.

1. What does the interviewer refer to by "that" as in "Why do you think that is"?
   a. Global warming was the threat of the 1980s.
   b. People seem to care about the threat of global warming no longer.

2. What does Dr. Clarke mean by "if so"?
   a. If scientists are engaged in the task of finding out about the global warming.
   b. If global warming is really happening.

3. What does Dr. Clarke refer to by "this" as in "because of this"?
   a. People's fear that the insulation might get thicker.
   b. The possibility that the insulation might get thicker.

4. What does the interviewer mean by "that" as in "Why is that"?
   a. The prediction is hard to verify.
   b. The prediction is precise.

5. What does the interviewer mean by "this" as in "And this avoids the sort of seasonal fluctuation of the temperature of land mass"?
   a. Measuring the temperature of the oceans as accurately as possible.
   b. Detecting the change in global temperature.

# Text Two

## I. Words and expressions

thermometer /θə'mɒmɪtə/ *n.* 温度计

buoy /bɔɪ/ *n.* 浮标
bob /bɒb/ *v.* 上下跳动
scan /skæn/ *v.* 扫描
radiometer /ˌreɪdɪˈɒmɪtə/ *n.* 辐射计
orbit /ˈɔːbɪt/ *v.* 绕轨道而行
infra-red /ˌɪnfrəˈred/ *n.* 红外线
detector /dɪˈtektə/ *n.* 检测器
intervene /ˌɪntəˈviːn/ *v.* 干涉

## II. Listen to confirm or to adjust

*Listen and find out if your expectations are the same as or different from what you hear. If different, find the correct one or ones from* ***Make your prediction****.*

## III. Listen and fill in the following blanks with the missing information.

*Main point I: Various ways of measuring the ocean temperature*

1. By placing ________________ in buoys and when ships draw water through their engines;
2. By ___________________;
3. By ________________, a radiometer which orbits the earth above us.

*Main point II: Advantages of using ATSR*

4. Greater ___________;
5. Large quantities of ___________;
6. Allows ______________ for it measures from two ______________;
7. A width of ______________;
8. Measures the temperature to ________________ centigrade.

## IV. Listen to some parts of the interview and complete the answers to the following questions.

1. What does "it" mean as in "we've measured it by placing …"?
   It refers to ________________________.
2. What did the interviewer mean by "this" as in "And what stage are you at with this"?
   The interviewer means __________________________.
3. What did Dr. Clarke mean by "this" as in "this is what we need"?
   Dr. Clarke means ________________.
4. What did Dr. Clarke refer to by "it" all the way through?
   It refers to ___________________.

## Part Three Look at This

### 联系邻近上下文，准确理解代词所指

口语与书面语相比有很多不同，其中包括对词汇量的要求相对较低，人们因此常以为口语更容易懂。确实，与书面语相比，口语中更频繁地使用一些常见高频词，包括各类代词，如 this，that，so，it 等，但是正是这些小词可能导致大问题。如果我们在听话时弄不清楚这些代词指代什么，那么即使没有生词或句法问题出现，我们仍然会不知所云。

明确代词所指关键在于紧密结合上下文，切忌断章取义。例如本课 Text One 中 Dr. Clarke 的这句话：

I think scientists have become occupied with the task of trying to find out whether it really is happening and, if so, whether it's caused by human activity.

虽然没有生词，但是要弄懂句子的意思，我们须弄清三个问题：

1. it really is happening 中的 it 是指什么？
2. if so 中的 so 是指什么？
3. whether it's caused by human activity 中的 it 是指什么？

于是我们需要借助上文：

**Interviewer:** Dr. Clarke, global warming was the threat of the 1980s but it seems to have fizzled out of people's minds — why do you think that is?

**Dr. Clarke:** Yes, in a way you're right ...

看了以上这段文字，我们知道：

1. it really is happening 中的 it 是指 global warming。
2. if so 中的 so 是指 global warming is really happening。
3. whether it's caused by human activity 中的 it 也是指 global warming。

我们在阅读时比较容易理解代词的所指，但听的时候则是另外一回事。因此平时要多听、多练习，增加对代词含义的敏感度。

一般而言，代词的含义主要可通过邻近的上下文找到，但也不排除一些特例，须联系整篇文章来理解，甚至涉及文中未提到但是通过常识可知的背景知识。本课着重练习借助邻近上下文推知关键代词的含义。

Part Four

## Here's More

### Exercise One

*Listen and answer the following questions.*

1. What does it mean by "it" as in "It's normal"?

   ______________________________

2. What does it mean by "it" as in "It's not spoiling a baby and it will not make a baby weak"?

   ______________________________

### Exercise Two

*Listen and complete the answers to the following questions.*

1. What does "ESL environment" mean?

   It means an environment where ______________.

2. What does "EFL environment" mean?

   It means an environment where English is not predominately the ______________.

### Exercise Three

*Listen and answer the following questions.*

1. What does the driver mean by "that" as in "that depends on the traffic"?

   ______________________________

2. Who is the driver referring to by "they" as in "they walk down the street looking straight up at the skyscrapers"?

   ______________________________

### Exercise Four

*Listen and complete the answers to the following questions.*

1. What is the father talking about when he asks "Did you receive it or not"?

   He is asking his daughter about her ______________.

2. What's the girl's problem with Spanish when she says "I got them all mixed up in my head"?

   She is saying that she was confused about the ______________ in Spanish.

# Unit 18

# China in Professor Evans's Eyes

## Part One Before You Listen

### I. Think and answer

1. Can you guess why some overseas people love to visit China?
2. In your opinion, what may most impress a foreign traveler when he/she first comes to China?
3. In recent years, China has developed tremendously. Can you list some of the changes around you?
4. What cultural differences or cultural shock may a foreign traveler encounter when visiting China?
5. Do you agree that the Chinese at home and those abroad are the same? If not, why?

### II. Make your prediction

*Browse through all the information offered in this unit and predict the main idea of Text One and Text Two by choosing from a, b, c and d. You may choose more than one answer to indicate your prediction.*

**Text One**

a. The places of interest Professor Evans has visited.
b. The reason why Professor Evans wants to come to China.
c. Professor Evans's first impression of China.
d. Some specific changes witnessed by Professor Evans in China.

### Text Two

a. Different kinds of Chinese people.
b. Professor Evans's ideas and suggestions on cultural shock.
c. The difference between the Chinese abroad and the Chinese at home.
d. The serious pollution issues in China.

## Part Two Listen Now

### Text One

#### I. Words and expressions

contribution /ˌkɒntrɪˈbjuːʃən/ *n.* 贡献
exceptional /ɪkˈsepʃənəl/ *adj.* 例外的；异常的；罕见的
densely /ˈdenslɪ/ *adv.* 稠密地；极度地
populate /ˈpɒpjʊleɪt/ *v.* 居住于
passage /ˈpæsɪdʒ/ *n.* (时间的)推移
outnumber /ˌaʊtˈnʌmbə/ *v.* 多于
densely populated 人口密集的
be destined to 注定

#### II. Listen to confirm or to adjust

*Listen and find out if your expectations are the same as or different from what you hear. If different, find the correct one or ones from **Make your prediction**.*

#### III. Listen and choose the best answer to each question you hear.

1. a. Because he is interested in Chinese history and language.
   b. Because he is retired.
   c. Because he has learned some Chinese.
   d. Because he wants to teach English.

2. a. Beijing International Airport.
   b. Large population.
   c. Heavy traffic.
   d. Both the large population and the huge public works.

3. a. More private cars.
   b. More highways.
   c. More people with an open mind.
   d. Fewer bikes.

## IV. Listen and decide whether the following statements are true (T) or false (F).

1. Professor Evans has been in Beijing for around three and a half years mainly because he is very much fascinated by Chinese culture, history and language. *T* ☐ *F* ☐
2. Beijing International Airport is large and well-equipped, just like many other international airports in the world. *T* ☐ *F* ☐
3. According to Professor Evans, there are more private cars than taxis in Shanghai recently. *T* ☐ *F* ☐
4. The problem of traffic jams will be eased in Shanghai if only more highways are built and more roads are widened. *T* ☐ *F* ☐
5. It is unwise to reduce the number of bikes because riding a bicycle can keep people healthy, cause no pollution and cost nothing. *T* ☐ *F* ☐
6. Professor Evans finds Chinese people are becoming more willing to accept new ideas and express their own opinions. *T* ☐ *F* ☐

# Text Two

## I. Words and expressions

custom /ˈkʌstəm/ *n.* 习俗；惯例
assume /əˈsjuːm/ *v.* (想当然地)认为
ethnically /ˈeθnɪkəlɪ/ *adv.* 人种上；种族上
privacy /ˈpraɪvəsɪ/ *n.* 隐私
value /ˈvæljuː/ *v.* 重视
illegal /ɪˈliːgəl/ *adj.* 非法的（反义词：legal）

immigrate /ˈɪmɪgreɪt/ *v.* (从外国)迁移入
immigrant /ˈɪmɪgrənt/ *n.* (外来)移民
menial /ˈmiːnɪəl/ *adj.* 卑贱的
predilection /ˌpriːdɪˈlekʃən/ *n.* 嗜好；偏爱
cultural shock 文化冲击

## II. Listen to confirm or to adjust

*Listen and find out if your expectations are the same as or different from what you hear. If different, find the correct one or ones from* ***Make your prediction****.*

## III. Listen and answer the following questions.

1. What is the greatest cultural shock Professor Evans has met in China?

______________________________________________

2. Why is it difficult to understand Americans?

______________________________________________

3. According to Professor Evans, what is the difference between the Chinese in the US and the Chinese at home?

______________________________________________

## IV. Listen and fill in the following blanks with the missing information.

1. Professor Evans may suggest other foreign visitors ________________ before coming to China so as not to suffer a lot from cultural shock. In fact, despite some cultural differences, he is very satisfied with his life in China, especially with ________________.
2. Unlike Chinese who like to stay with many others, Americans prefer to be alone because they are more individualistic and emphasize ________________.
3. Many Chinese people have got many dreams about the US. But when they live there for some time, they quickly realize that the US is ________________, where they have to ________________ than they did in China. Therefore some of them even think about going back to China because ________________.

## Part Three Look at This

### 熟悉并把握信号词以跟上讲话人的思路

在语言交流中，信号词可以承上启下，表明说话人的思路以及句子之间乃至整个语篇的逻辑关系。因此，通过留心信号词，我们可以捕捉到重要的信息和数据，把握说话人的思路，并及时调整预测，分清主次。请看出现在本单元采访中的句子：

1. Ever since I took some courses in college about Chinese history and Chinese language, I've been interested in China. *So* when I retired I decided to come to China…(So 表示此句与前一句为因果关系，即 Professor Evans 来中国的原因是对中国的历史和语言感兴趣。)

2. Actually I didn't suffer from a large cultural shock, because I did a lot of preparation before I came. *But* some things you just cannot prepare for.(But 表示此句与前面一句为转折关系，即尽管可以作些准备，但准备工作无法面面俱到。于是我们可以猜测下文中会提到一些事先无法预料的事情。)

对于信号词，我们可以作如下分类：

1. 表示因果：so，because，since，altogether，finally，as a result，now that 等；
2. 表示转折或对比：yet，but，however，although，by contrast，as a matter of fact 等；
3. 表示递进或补充：in addition (to)，besides，and，another thing 等；
4. 表示顺序或序列：first，first of all，then，second，before，after 等；
5. 表示强调或解释：I mean，that is，in particular 等。

## Part Four Here's More

### Exercise

*You will hear ten short conversations with some "signal" words or phrases. Listen and choose the best answer to each question you hear.*

1. a. He and his wife enjoyed the play.
   b. He enjoyed the play but his wife didn't.

c. Neither of them enjoyed the play.
d. His wife enjoyed the play, but he didn't.

2. a. 800,000.
b. 813,000.
c. 813,400.
d. 831,400.

3. a. He shouldn't borrow the hand calculator.
b. He shouldn't keep the calculator on between problems.
c. He shouldn't turn the calculator off between problems.
d. He shouldn't use the battery.

4. a. They love shopping very much.
b. They will buy something first.
c. They have had a good time in Shanghai.
d. They have just arrived in Shanghai.

5. a. The UK.
b. The US.
c. Australia.
d. Austria.

6. a. Tommy can't hear very well.
b. Tommy never smokes.
c. Tommy never listens to her.
d. Tommy goes out before she says anything to him.

7. a. Because her mother asked her to charge more.
b. Because she is a good baby sitter.
c. Because she does some housework while the parents are out.
d. Because it is difficult to find a baby sitter on Friday.

8. a. To be on holiday.
b. To complete his course requirements.
c. To get a job.
d. To enroll in a teacher's training course.

9. a. He loves his shirt.
b. He doesn't like Linda.
c. He won't buy a birthday present for Linda.
d. He always plays poker for money.

10. a. Somewhere that is within a short driving distance to campus.
b. A place where she can live alone.
c. An apartment at a rent of $200 exclusively.
d. An apartment with furniture already in it.

# Unit 19

# Spring Festival and Christmas

## Part One Before You Listen

### I. Think and answer

1. According to your knowledge, how do people in Western countries celebrate Christmas?
2. Christmas is becoming more and more popular in China, especially among young people. What do you think of the phenomenon?
3. How do Chinese people celebrate the Spring Festival?
4. Have you ever received any gift for Christmas or the Spring Festival? If so, can you tell about the most impressive one?
5. In what aspects are Christmas and the Spring Festival similar to or different from each other?

### II. Make your prediction

*Browse through all the information offered in this unit and predict the main idea of Text One and Text Two by choosing from a, b, c and d. You may choose more than one answer to indicate your prediction.*

#### Text One

a. Professor Evans's celebration of Christmas in China.

b. The most memorial gift received by Professor Evans in China.

c. Professor Evans's comments on the popularity of Christmas in China.

d. An interesting Christmas story related by Professor Evans.

**Text Two**

a. Professor Evans's first impression of the Chinese New Year.
b. Professor Evans's unpleasant memories about the Spring Festival.
c. A comparison and contrast made by Professor Evans between Christmas and the Spring Festival.
d. Professor Evans's feelings about the Spring Festival.

# Listen Now

## Text One

### I. Words and expressions

Christ /kraɪst/ *n.* 基督
Christian /'krɪstjən/ *n.* 基督教徒
Bible /'baɪbl/ *n.* 基督教《圣经》
verse /vɜːs/ *n.* (《圣经》中的)节，句
hymn /hɪm/ *n.* (尤指基督教的)赞美诗，圣歌
symbolize /'sɪmbəlaɪz/ *v.* 作为……的象征
humanity /hjuː'mænətɪ/ *n.* 人类；(总称)人
phenomenon /fɪ'nɒmɪnən/ *n.* 现象
Santa Claus /'sæntəˌklɔːz/ 圣诞老人

### II. Listen to confirm or to adjust

*Listen and find out if your expectations are the same as or different from what you hear. If different, find the correct one or ones from* ***Make your prediction****.*

### III. Listen and choose the best answer to complete each of the following sentences.

1. An ideal celebration of Christmas includes ________.

a. attending the ceremony held by church
b. having a large meal with family and opening gifts
c. hanging stockings filled with lots of toys
d. both *a* and *b*

2. The greatest Christmas gift Professor Evans has received in China is ________.
   a. getting some time to fly back to the US
   b. having some friends come to Shanghai to visit him
   c. having some relatives come to China and spend Christmas with him
   d. getting an air ticket for free

3. Professor Evans is ________ when talking about the commercialization of Christmas in China.
   a. optimistic
   b. critical
   c. pessimistic
   d. happy

## IV. Listen and decide whether the following statements are true (T) or false (F).

| | T | F |
|---|---|---|
| 1. Christmas was first celebrated by Christians for the birth of Jesus. | T □ | F □ |
| 2. According to Professor Evans, American people prefer to spend Christmas Eve noisily. | T □ | F □ |
| 3. On Christmas Day, children are always happy to read Bible verses, sing holy songs and receive gifts such as toys, candy and fruit filled in stockings. | T □ | F □ |
| 4. For many Chinese people, Christmas just means lots of cards and gifts, beautiful Christmas decorations and kind Santa Clause. | T □ | F □ |
| 5. Professor Evans believes that non-Christians can also completely understand Christmas and appreciate it. | T □ | F □ |
| 6. In Professor Evans's opinion, Christmas has become more like a business now and is losing its real meaning gradually. | T □ | F □ |

# Text Two

## I. Words and expressions

highlight /ˈhaɪlaɪt/ *n.* 最精彩的时刻（或细节）

superficial /ˌsjuːpəˈfɪʃəl/ *adj.* 表面的；肤浅的
firecracker /ˈfaɪəˌkrækə/ *n.* 爆竹，鞭炮
skyrocket /ˈskaɪˌrɒkɪt/ *n.* 冲天火箭(一种焰火)
sacrifice /ˈsækrɪfaɪs/ *n.* (因奉献而)牺牲
glutinous /ˈgluːtɪnəs/ *adj.* 粘的

## II. Listen to confirm or to adjust

*Listen and find out if your expectations are the same as or different from what you hear. If different, find the correct one or ones from **Make your prediction**.*

## III. Listen and match the festivals in Column I with the descriptions in Column II.

| Column I | Column II |
|---|---|
| 1. Christmas<br>(　　　　　　　　) | a. For it, people would travel long distances to go back home. |
| | b. It has a tradition of giving gifts. |
| | c. It stresses the idea of eating big meals together. |
| 2. The Spring Festival<br>(　　　　　　　　) | d. People would travel with their families during it. |
| | e. People would play a lot of fireworks to celebrate it. |
| | f. People would take on a new look for it. |
| | g. People would cook big dinners together to celebrate it. |
| | h. People would have a big house cleaning and pay off debts before it. |
| | i. During it, people would reflect and pray quietly and give thanks to each other. |
| | j. It is a symbol of a new start of the next year. |
| | k. It is a religious festival. |
| | l. People would prepare a lot of different pork dishes for it as well as other traditional food. |

## IV. Listen and answer the following questions.

1. How does Professor Evans feel about his experiences during the Spring Festival in his Chinese friends' homes?

______________________________________________

2. On what level do Christmas and the Spring Festival differ from each other?

______________________________________________

3. Why does Professor Evans respect those standing fast to their position during the Spring Festival?

______________________________

4. What traditional Spring Festival foods has Professor Evans mentioned?

______________________________

5. Why has Professor Evans been struck most by the eating of pork?

______________________________

6. Was Professor Evans wearing a lot of clothes when he first stayed with a Chinese family for the Spring Festival?

______________________________

## Part Three Look at This

### 美国的宗教

每年的12月25日是西方的圣诞节，也是全世界基督教徒的传统节日。在美国，超过一半的人口信奉基督教(Christianity)。基督教又分为天主教(Roman Catholicism)、东正教(Eastern Orthodoxy)和新教(Protestantism)。在美国，天主教徒(Roman Catholic)一般是爱尔兰人、意大利人和波兰人的后代；新教徒(Protestant)人数最多，占全体基督教徒的58%；东正教徒(Orthodox)人数最少，主要分布在美国的东部、中西部和加利福尼亚。事实上，由于早期的美国移民中新教徒占大多数，所以在当时还曾存在针对从意大利和爱尔兰移民来的天主教徒的宗教歧视。

除了基督教外，在美国还存在着许多不同的教派和信仰，例如犹太教(Judaism)、伊斯兰教(Islam)、佛教(Buddhism)、印度教(Hinduism)等等。

## Part Four Here's More

### Exercise One

*Listen and decide whether the following statements are true (T) or false (F).*

1. The first English immigrants came to New England for freedom of belief. *T* ☐ *F* ☐
2. Religion has little influence on the government in the United States. *T* ☐ *F* ☐
3. Although there are many different religions in the United States, most American people believe in Christianity or Judaism. *T* ☐ *F* ☐
4. Both Christians and Jews believe there is one God and celebrate Christmas and Easter. *T* ☐ *F* ☐
5. For Jews, the weekly Holy Day is from Friday morning to Saturday morning. *T* ☐ *F* ☐
6. Traditional religion has become deemphasized in the United States since 1950s. So religion is not providing customs or ceremonies now. *T* ☐ *F* ☐
7. In the US, churches do not only play the traditional role in the society now. *T* ☐ *F* ☐

## Exercise Two

*Listen to a short paragraph for three times and take a dictation.*

______________________________________________

______________________________________________

______________________________________________

______________________________________________

______________________________________________

______________________________________________

# Unit 20

# Teaching English to Chinese University Students

## Part One Before You Listen

### I. Think and answer

1. What is your grasp of English like?
2. Should we learn some cultural knowledge while learning English? Why?
3. In your opinion, what is the main problem when Chinese learn English?
4. Can you tell why Chinese students are usually passive in class?
5. There are many differences between Chinese students and American students. Can you list some?

### II. Make your prediction

*Browse through all the information offered in this unit and predict the main idea of Text One and Text Two by choosing from a, b, c and d. You may choose more than one answer to indicate your prediction.*

#### Text One

a. Chinese students' strengths in English learning.
b. Language itself and culture in language teaching and learning.
c. Students' preference for cultural knowledge in language learning.
d. Suggestions to Chinese learners of English.

### Text Two

a. Active and creative American students.
b. Large Chinese classes.
c. The reasons why Chinese students are passive in class.
d. The differences between Chinese and American students.

## Part Two Listen Now

### Text One

#### I. Words and expressions

consequently /ˈkɒnsɪkwəntlɪ/ *adv.* 结果，因此
attach /əˈtætʃ/ *v.* 装上；贴上；系上；附加
inseparable /ɪnˈsepərəbl/ *adj.* 不可分离的；不可分割的
hesitancy /ˈhezɪtənsɪ/ *n.* 迟疑，犹豫
East China Normal University 华东师范大学

#### II. Listen to confirm or to adjust

*Listen and find out if your expectations are the same as or different from what you hear. If different, find the correct one or ones from **Make your prediction**.*

#### III. Listen and choose the best answer to each question you hear.

1. a. Their basic grasp of English grammar and Western culture.
   b. Their ability to make sentences.
   c. Their ability to learn new vocabulary fast.
   d. Their weak speaking and listening skills.

2. a. Culture knowledge is more important than language itself.
   b. Culture knowledge is less important than language itself.
   c. Culture knowledge is closely related to language itself.

d. Culture knowledge can be separated from language itself.

3. a. Chinese students should relax when speaking English.
   b. Chinese students should be brave in making mistakes when speaking English.
   c. Chinese students should take every chance to talk to people in English.
   d. Chinese students should try to learn more English grammar.

## IV. Listen and answer the following questions.

1. What does Professor Evans teach at East China Normal University?

   ______________________________

2. What does Professor Evans stress in his classes?

   ______________________________

3. Why do the students try to experience American culture through Professor Evans?

   ______________________________

4. What is the most common problem among Chinese learners of English?

   ______________________________

# Text Two

## I. Words and expressions

participation /pɑːˌtɪsɪˈpeɪʃən/ *n.* 参与
subdued /səbˈdʒuːd/ *adj.* 被制服的；顺从的
fundamental /ˌfʌndəˈmentəl/ *adj.* 基础的；十分重要的；主要的
authority /ɔːˈθɒrətɪ/ *n.* 权威；权威人士
experimentation /ɪkˌsperɪmenˈteɪʃən/ *n.* 实验，试验
passive /ˈpæsɪv/ *adj.* 被动的；消极的；顺从的
beget /bɪˈget/ *v.* 引起，招致
stimulate /ˈstɪmjʊleɪt/ *v.* 刺激；促使，起促进作用
orthodoxy /ˈɔːθədɒksɪ/ *n.* 正统做法；正统观念；正统派的学说
mature /məˈtʃʊə/ *v.* 变成熟
complicated /ˈkɒmplɪkeɪtɪd/ *adj.* 复杂的；难懂的
drop out 退出

## II. Listen to confirm or to adjust

*Listen and find out if your expectations are the same as or different from what you hear. If different, find the correct one or ones from* ***Make your prediction****.*

## III. Listen and choose the best answer to each question you hear.

1. a. They don't have a chance to speak out.
   b. They aren't encouraged to speak out.
   c. They prefer taking notes to speaking out.
   d. They don't like asking questions.
2. a. American students are more willing to speak out and share ideas with other people than Chinese students.
   b. American students are more active than Chinese students.
   c. American students can enjoy much more flexibility of their education than Chinese students.
   d. American students spend more money on their education than Chinese students.
3. a. Some of them work during the winter and summer holidays.
   b. It's not easy for them to change their majors.
   c. Most of them do not start to work until they graduate from school.
   d. They seldom listen to their parents.

## IV. Listen and fill in the following blanks with the missing information.

1. In China, students have been taught to ______________________________, to ______________________________ and not to speak out actively. Therefore, they write down everything said by teachers and seldom ____________________. In fact, according to Professor Evans, this can be explained by a long-standing tradition of Chinese education in which people are required to learn by observation and ______________________ instead of __________, ___________ or experimentation.
2. According to Professor Evans, American teachers usually encourage their students to share ideas with other people because ________________________________________. Although sometimes it may cause a waste of time, particularly when ______________________________, it can still make students ______________ and be creative.
3. According to Professor Evans, Chinese students can express their ideas quite well but most of them tend ________________________. Seemingly, they don't want to stand out to challenge orthodoxy or ______________________________.
4. Sometimes American students may choose to work first and then come back to study

probably because they ______________________________________ or just ____________ ______________________________ before continuing their education.

## Part Three Look at This

### 理解话语的隐含意义

有时候，出于某种原因，说话人会较隐晦或含蓄地表达自己的意思。在这种情况下，听者对话语的理解就不能只停留在字面上，而需要根据上下文理解隐含的意义。在本单元的采访中我们曾听到以下这些话里藏话的句子：

1. I think, broadly speaking, that is correct. There are limits, of course. It depends on the teacher, for one thing. (根据上文，我们可以推断出讲话人的意思是 American students are not always encouraged to speak out by their teachers。)

2. So this flexibility is, I think, one of the strong points of American education. In China, it is much more difficult for students to change directions. (根据前面的句子，我们可以推断出后一句的意思是 Chinese education is not so flexible as American education。)

要了解话语的隐含意义，需要根据特定的语境(如前后的词语和句子)、说话者的语气等进行积极听辨和思考。比如在以上第一句中，讲话人先肯定这个观点在广义上是正确的，但接下来话锋一转，说它当然有局限，比如那要看老师怎么教，潜台词是并非所有老师都鼓励学生这么做。再看以上第二句，讲话人先说灵活性是美国教育的一大优点，接着便说中国学生相对较难改变方向，潜台词是中国教育不如美国教育那样灵活。可见要理解话语中的潜台词，必须抓住关键词和细节来推断。

## Part Four Here's More

### Exercise

*You will hear a number of statements with implied meaning. Choose the answer which is the closest in meaning to the statement you hear.*

1. a. Mathew is good at playing tennis.
   b. Mathew is enthusiastic about his new course.
   c. Mathew is not interested in his schoolwork.
   d. Mathew spends a lot of time on study.

2. a. It's easy to forecast weather.
   b. The heat wave will stay for a while.
   c. The hot weather is about to end.
   d. The weather forecast is not reliable.

3. a. I'd love to have dinner with you.
   b. I'd love to do my history paper.
   c. I'm afraid I can't have dinner with you.
   d. I'm busy with my study.

4. a. Miss Smith is good at singing.
   b. Miss Smith didn't know how to sing "Home, Sweet home."
   c. Miss Smith sang "Home, Sweet home" very badly.
   d. Miss Smith seldom sings publicly.

5. a. You'd better ask for a reduction in your rent.
   b. You will eventually decide to stay in the dormitory.
   c. You need to rent a cheap apartment.
   d. I will find out the cost of living in an apartment.

6. a. Mitchell didn't accept that job offer because of the low pay.
   b. Mitchell refused the job because of the hours.
   c. The job didn't provide a good working environment.
   d. The job was not challenging at all.

7. a. I haven't seen the paintings yet.
   b. I don't like our art history class.
   c. I don't like those paintings.
   d. I will buy one painting for you.

8. a. You should buy a vacuum cleaner.

b. Your parents should come after this weekend.

c. Your apartment is dirty and you should do some cleaning.

d. You should take your parents somewhere else.

9. a. It may be difficult for George to work and study at the same time.

b. George is teaching in school this summer.

c. George is working very hard so that he can afford to go to New York.

d. George will not go to New York this summer.

10. a. The financial situation is better than people have expected.

b. If you hadn't explained it so well, the financial situation would seem worse.

c. The financial situation wouldn't seem any worse if you explained it properly.

d. The financial situation can't be any worse than you've made it sound.

# Appendix I
# Listening Scripts

## Unit 1 Clothes

### Part Two Listen Now

#### Text One

**Interviewer:** Hi, Barbara. You look wonderful in this dress.

**Barbara:** Thank you very much.

**Interviewer:** I've found that most women professors wear dresses in class.

**Barbara:** Yes, I think that they do. They wear dresses or skirts and blouses, suits maybe. Aah ... or sweaters and skirts. Aah ... I also think that they sometimes wear slacks because in the winter it is very cold here, and so nice wool slacks sometimes feel very comfortable and warm.

**Interviewer:** Do people wear different clothes on different occasions?

**Barbara:** Yes, of course, they do. Um ... on more formal occasions, people have clothes that they probably save for special occasions, aah ... like going to church, you might, people might, women might have a special dress that they wear, aah ... and jewelry like a necklace or um earrings and rings, special things that they kind of save for church.

**Interviewer:** I think weddings are also regarded as very formal occasions.

**Barbara:** Exactly. And for a wedding, for instance, my son is getting married in May, women usually wear the most formal, that might be one of the most formal occasions; men wear tuxedoes. And I'll be wearing a long dress. It's actually long with the straight skirt and has some sequins and um beads sewn around the midriff to make it very special. And I'll probably wear a corsage, a little flower corsage, and a pearl necklace and earrings. And there're other formal occasions, too, dances maybe, or special parties where people do have special dresses that they wear that are very fancy.

**Interviewer:** So women wear special dresses while men tuxedoes. Then what do most people wear on informal occasions?

**Barbara:** For informal occasions, um ... there're a lot of informal events, like sports events or family get-togethers or shopping, where people usually, women usually wear slacks, sometimes they wear jeans, aah ... aah knit shirts, cotton shirts or blouses, sweaters, anything that's very comfortable and allows free movement.

**III. Listen and choose the best answer to each question you hear.**

1. Which of the following is NOT usually worn on a formal occasion?
2. On an informal occasion, what kind of clothes do people prefer to wear?
3. Which of the following will Barbara NOT wear when she attends her son's wedding?

## Text Two

**Interviewer:** Is it true that the kind of clothes people wear indicates their social status and the job they do?

**Barbara:** Yes, I think that's true to some extent, anyway. I think it used to be more true. Aah ... in, in recent years, I think there has been a trend toward less formality at work.

**Interviewer:** You mean people don't dress as formally as before?

**Barbara:** Yes, but there still is a definite status associated with certain kinds of clothes, like men wear suits and ties. Aah ... that's a definite example. For instance, my son works in human relations or human resource area. When he worked at the central office, he always wore a suit and a tie. And now he is in a subsidiary office, in Portland, Oregon. It's a more casual working environment. He ... it's a manufacturing plant, and so he tends to wear shirts and casual pants rather than a suit every day to work.

**Interviewer:** So it depends. By the way, do most people buy their clothes or make them themselves?

**Barbara:** Most people buy their clothes. Aah ... I enjoy making some of my clothes. I used to do more of it than I do now. My latest project is making a dress for the flower girl on my son's wedding. That's kind of fun, it's a fun sewing project. And I do make my own clothes because I find that it's more economical and it's kind of a creative project for me. But I would say most people do not make their own clothes.

**Interviewer:** OK. So what kind of clothes are in fashion now, do you think?

**Barbara:** Well, I recently read that colors for next year are going to be red, beige, navy and grey, and no black. For a long time, black seemed to be a very popular, important color. Everyone needed to have a black dress. So I thought that was an interesting combination of colors. Um ... but I would say that the fashion trends … aah … have a very wide range that people tend these days to wear what they prefer, what they enjoy, wearing aah ... um ... what makes them feel good and so I don't know if there're any particular fashion trends, at least for women that I can aah ... pinpoint right at the moment.

## Part Four Here's More

## Exercise

1. I would say … I mean some people, no, most people buy their clothes. But I enjoy making my clothes, I mean some of my clothes.
2. For a long time, everyone seemed to be, black seemed to be a very popular, important color. Everyone liked, I mean everyone needed to have a black dress for some occasions.

3. You want to go to the fashion show? Let me see. It's two blocks away, no, no, three blocks away. Walk till you go to the traffic lights and then turn left, no, turn right. The fashion show is there and you can't miss it.
4. And um … we usually sit together and talk first, and serve um … maybe something to drink.
5. And all of these are very, seem like very individualistic uh … reasons for divorcing.
6. Bus travel is, aah … tends to be the cheapest form of transportation.
7. But then perhaps they are much more, they tend to be more adventuresome.
8. So I often talk about, often in my language classes, include a lot of culture, cultural knowledge.
9. Perhaps I shouldn't say it's a problem, I should ... it's a phenomenon.
10. Many people don't, they are not able to be with their families.
11. Of course, this can also tend to be somewhat time-wasting if the ideas, if there are not any important ideas that are brought up.
12. Those kinds of, they look for those kinds of similarities.
13. And just there's, it seems like in America there's something for everyone, of all different economic uh … groups.
14. So in the winter time, people when they retire, they like to have um … they like to go down south in warmer climate.
15. And they might … they must be … have some pride and be involved in the profession and to share their profession with others.

## Part Two Listen Now

### Text One

**Interviewer:** Hello, Barbara, the pumpkin pie you made tastes so good. How did you do it?

**Barbara:** Well, thank you. Aah ... pumpkin pie is a kind of traditional dessert that we make for Thanksgiving. It goes along with other special things that we serve for Thanksgiving like turkey and ... and other foods. Pumpkin pie is … is kind of challenge to make any kind of pie. A good cook is known for how good the crust she makes on … on various pies, apple pie or pumpkin pie.

**Interviewer:** How do you make the crust?

**Barbara:** You make a crust by mixing together flour, shortening, a little salt and a little water, and you use a pastry blender which is some wires that are attached together to kind of cut the shortening into the flour. That's what makes the crust, our pastry aah … um very flaky and tender. So you make, you make the pastry, you push it into, aah … roll it out and put it in a pie plate and then you mix pumpkin and eggs, and milk and many spices: cinnamon and nutmeg, sugar together.

**Interviewer:** So a lot of ingredients.

**Barbara:** Ya. And you make a custard kind of, you pour it into a pie crust, on top of the crust in the pan. And then you bake that about an hour at a low temperature. And it is a delicious dessert.

**Interviewer:** You sound a remarkable cook. Do you cook meals for your family?

**Barbara:** Aah ... yes, I do. Um ... my family now just consists of my husband and I because our two sons're grown. So um ... my cooking is not as extensive as I was when I had children at home. But I do make, aah ... dinner every night. And my husband and I have dinner together every evening. Aah ... I prepare a variety of types of meals for dinner, um ...

**Interviewer:** Does it take very long for you to cook a meal?

**Barbara:** It takes about, ya, about half an hour to an hour for me to make a meal. And on weekends, I might do something more extensive. It might, I might be cooking for a couple of hours, but usually um ... I try to do things that're very simple because I do work all day and by the time I get home in the evening I am tired.

## Text Two

**Interviewer:** What do people usually eat for breakfast, lunch and dinner?

**Barbara:** For breakfast, they usually eat, maybe dry cereal or hot cereal and milk, fruit, aah ... maybe some toast with jam, coffee and juice. Aah ... if you're going to have a, a big breakfast, people might eat eggs: scrambled eggs or fried eggs, and pancakes perhaps.

**Interviewer:** And what for lunch?

**Barbara:** For lunch, I think, aah ... some very popular things would be sandwiches and different soups. And then for dinner, there is a whole variety of kinds of foods that people eat. I do a lot of stir-fry cooking, where I put vegetables and meat together. And I pay attention to trying to get nutritious meals so that we eat foods from all of the food groups like vegetables and fruits, cereals and breads, milk and milk products, and then protein from meat or eggs, and different cheeses, too.

**Interviewer:** So you seem to pay a lot of attention to dinner.

**Barbara:** I do, because it's the one time when my husband and I relax together and we have a chance to talk. Um ... and we probably eat kind of hurried meals through the day. So this is probably our most nutritious meal and most relaxing meal of the day.

**Interviewer:** By the way, do you sometimes entertain guests at home?

**Barbara:** Yes, we do. Um ... very often if I do entertain guests at home, it is for dinner. And so I invite people over for dinner. Sometimes on a very informal basis. It might be family, where we have a picnic and maybe even eat outdoors and cook um ... different, maybe chicken on the grill.

**Interviewer:** This, I guess, happens in fine and warm weather. In winter ...

**Barbara:** Um ... then in, in winter, particularly we maybe have more formal dinners, when we invite people to our home. And um ... we usually sit together and talk first, and serve um ... maybe something to drink. And then aah ... we have our meal which consists of maybe soup at first or salad, and then a main dish. It could be a casserole; it could be a stir-fry dish; it could be a roast, um ... and vegetables and fruit and salad. And then I usually serve a dessert. And we sit around the table and talk, and have dessert and coffee, and just relax, spend a lot of time talking. And then that usually consists of our formal occasion.

**Interviewer:** So on a formal occasion, I think maybe aah ... there're rules for you to lay the table. For example, to put the forks and spoons in certain places.

**Barbara:** I actually do spend a little bit of thought on how I set the table. I use a nice tablecloth, maybe have candles or flowers on the table. And um ... we do set our plates and utensils in certain ways. We put, place the fork on the left side of the plate on top of the napkin. And then we place the knife, sharp side in on the right side and the spoon next to the knife. And then we put the water glass just above the knife at the top of the plate. And there might be other glasses like wine glass, so we put it at the center at the top of the plate. And so this is just kind of the way that people set a formal table.

**Interviewer:** Thank you, Barbara, for spending your time telling me so much.

## Part Four Here's More

### Exercise One

**Passage One Is Your Bathtub Discolored?**

It's probably hard water stains. What to do? Try to cover the tub in paper towels, and soak them in full strength vinegar. After a couple of hours, remove the soaked towels and presto! Your tub will look like new.

**Passage Two Clean Blankets with a Professional Look**

If your blankets can be machine washed, here's a way to have them looking at their best. Before washing the blanket, set the cycle, add the detergent and let the machine fill. When all the soap is dissolved, add the blanket. Let it soak, and then wash on gentle. In the final rinse, add 1-1/2 cups of white vinegar. It will give your blanket a clean smell, and give it a little fluff.

### Exercise Two

**Passage One Try This Recipe for Some "Play Clay"**

Heat 2-1/2 cups of salt and 1 cup of water until just boiling. Then mix 1-1/2 cups of cornstarch with 3/4 cup of water. Add this to the salt and water mixture. Stir until it is thick. If necessary, add more water or cornstarch for consistency. Stir until it is thick. Cool and store it in the refrigerator.

**Passage Two How to Remove Candle Wax from the Carpet**

Scrape off as much wax as you can, using a table knife. Then cover the spot with paper toweling and iron the spot (synthetic setting). The napkin will show through wax. Remove and repeat until all the wax is lifted from the carpet.

# Unit 3 Real Estate

## Part Two Listen Now

### Text One

**Interviewer:** Mrs. Johnson, how long have you been a real estate agent?

**Mrs. Johnson:** Uh ... I've been an agent since 1981. And um ... it was a bad year to go into real estate because the interest rates in America were uh ... 17 and 18% for mortgage whereas now they're like 6 and 7 and 8% which makes homes more affordable than they were then.

**Interviewer:** So it was a tough time to get in.

**Mrs. Johnson:** It was. And every year uh ... in order to keep my license, I have to uh ... take 15 hours of continuing education, uh ... pay my license fee, uh ... also pay my association dues to the uh ... Professional Association of Southern Twin Cities, Association of Realtors, state association and the National Association of Realtors. And in addition to that, now it's becoming more and more necessary to invest in your company. Uh ... you're an independent contractor as a realtor, you don't get a salary. You only get a percentage of the, uh ... of the, of the fee that sellers are charged for marketing their homes.

**Interviewer:** So you don't have a regular income. And it completely depends on the selling.

**Mrs. Johnson:** You're right. And the broker keeps some of your shares of the fee with, maybe, another brokerage because maybe you listed, maybe the other company sold. So uh ... that's where your income comes from, something like 1.5% of the uh ... 6% perhaps. That is charged for the seller of house, of the marketing of the house. And more and more you're going, you need to, you have to have a computer, you have to have, the more you have, the better you're going to be at it because people are very impressed when you do listing presentation, if you have a laptop computer, and you can call up. Also it's a fact and statistics to show them how, how much their house could sell for in today's market.

**Interviewer:** It sounds very essential.

**Mrs. Johnson:** Ya. And also if you're working with some buyer, you can, uh ... there're software programs. You can pull up uh ... one is called "Know your neighborhood, " that I just heard about. And you can just pull up anything about any neighborhood in the whole country, and the street that you might want to live on. Or whatever you can see, where the houses are sold and what the prices, you know, what they paid for those houses. And also it's for information about community, the schools and transportation and uh ... average income.

**Interviewer:** It's getting very high tech.

**Mrs. Johnson:** But the average realtor does not have enough money to buy those things. They choose not to. Only the ones that are super successful seem to feel that they can afford to spend another thousand dollars a year upgrading their technological aspects of their business.

**Interviewer:** You mean not everyone in your area is successful.

**Mrs. Johnson:** Definitely.

**Interviewer:** So your job is kind to connect the seller and the buyer. And would you please uh ... tell the whole process how you help sellers to sell their houses and buyers to buy what they want?

**Mrs. Johnson:** Well, in helping a seller sell their houses, first of all, the most important thing is uh ... pricing the house at a fair market value. And if you don't price it right, then it's too high and people, when they're looking for houses, say, "This house doesn't give me uh ... as much for the money as that house over there that I've just looked at." So your job is to help the sellers understand that they, they must price their house based on, on market value, what, what it would sell for today.

**Interviewer:** How do you manage to know the market value?

**Mrs. Johnson:** We come to that conclusion by comparing all previous sales within the last six months, to the, as close as possible to the same type of house that they're interested in selling. And what buyers are willing to pay is actually what determines uh ... what the selling cost would be. And we try to guide them into that favorable market position.

**Interviewer:** Is it possible that a seller thinks that his or her house could be priced higher than you've told?

**Mrs. Johnson:** Um ... sometimes they think that they should get more than they, than the market indicates. And that causes some uh ... problems for realtors because if you put an unrealistic price on a house, it's just going to sit there and sit there and not sell. And then the sellers would be unhappy. So the, to really be uh ... helpful to your sellers, you help them establish the right market price for their house, help them to uh ... see things about their house they can fix up before the sale and before they start, before we would start to show it to the public. Um ... and we call that staging your house.

**Interviewer:** Staging the house?

**Mrs. Johnson:** We might go through the whole house with the seller and help them rearrange the house, get rid of the clutter, pack up all the junk in the closet that isn't necessary. And if you have too much stuff, even rent space to store it so that the house doesn't look uh ... too small and crowded, so that it looks very neat. Certain rooms may need painting or if you needs some special work, and the landscaping, the realtor has an eye for the sort of thing. And he or she will tell the seller that this really should be done in order to present your house in the best possible light.

## Text Two

**Interviewer:** What is the average price of a house in this area?

**Mrs. Johnson:** OK. Um ... I brought some statistics with me. We got it briefly from our computer. And um ... the average price of a ... I would say the medium price, sell price of a house would be uh ... $140,000. And the house might list for $144,000. But it would probably more than likely sell for $140,000. That's a possibility. Or if the market is tight, it could sell for 144,000. But I'll say that it'll sell for 140,000. That would um ... pretty much be a house that had 1,848 square feet and would be built perhaps in 1994. And it would have 4 bedrooms and 2 or 3 bathrooms.

**Interviewer:** What kind of house? One or two storied?

**Mrs. Johnson:** Perhaps a rambler. That means all, most of the living space would be on one level. And that would usually include a basement and a double garage for that price. Uh ... the listings, I have listing prices for various prices of different types of property. The average listing price for a condo town house in our small town is $121,000. And the average listing price for a hobby farm or an active farm uh ... according to our market is $271,737. And the average time on market for that would be 85 days. The average time on the market for the condo town house would be 105 days before it would be sold.

**Interviewer:** So a condo town house takes longer time.

**Mrs. Johnson:** Ya. Then um ... we have like 3 um ... investment listings. The average listing price for investment would be $313,300. And the average market time of course will go up then because it's hard to sell a higher price property. That would be 269 days. (And um ... here, that's it because it gives you the rest of them.)

**Interviewer:** What is the percentage of people who can afford to buy this kind of house whose price you've mentioned?

**Mrs. Johnson:** Hum. OK. I say that uh ... probably uh ... something like 90 to 95% of the people could afford property in this area. And the rest then would uh ... would be renting. And then there're 3 or 4 different ways they could rent. Uh ... there would be government-assisted housing for the needy. And the government would, the state and the federal and the local government would contribute toward the uh ... the rental, uh ... in the low interest rental of a smaller apartment, but it would have, uh ... you know, good running water, toilets and a good kitchen and would be very livable, and not substandard it would be, really quality housing. Um ... below that would be, it could be above it or below it, sometimes people would, um ... would want to maybe buy their own ... rent a mobile house in ... in a mobile park. And they can be expensive or they can be inexpensive.

**Interviewer:** It depends on what?

**Mrs. Johnson:** It depends on how rundown they are. Some of them aren't in real good shape so it would be less expensive, but affordable to people who need them. And then there are some that are very uh ... um ... pricey. But a lot of them are, you know, below, way below 100,000. I mean 40,000, you can get a brand new one. I have a realtor friend whose husband is retired and just recently she's thinking of retiring from real estate. She has a daughter in Florida. And so she and her husband bought a double wide mobile house uh ... for 12,000 dollars.

**Interviewer:** Was it a new one?

**Mrs. Johnson:** Naturally it wasn't new but she is used, they're used to having nice housing, so it was good housing. And just there's, it seems like in America there's something for everyone, of all different economics uh ... groups. So I was very pleased to hear that another of my friends bought a condo in Arizona for, this is just for the second house. I forgot to mention that. That's a second house, uh ... for going .... We live in a cooler, cold climate. So in the winter, people when they retire, they like to have um ... they like to go down south in warmer climate. They either rent down south which is kind of, expen ... can be kind of expensive or they buy, which uh ... my other friend bought a condo in Arizona for 30,000. But I also have friends who bought, who had the second home built, who are doctors or lawyers, who have paid 300,000 dollars.

**Interviewer:** OK. There's really something for everyone.

**Mrs. Johnson:** (Laugh) So there's a wide variety and you know, can go, it can go quite ways higher than that, too. But I haven't heard of any that is as good deal as my realtor friend made this year at 12,000 dollars for double wide for their second home. That was, that tops it. And they do have monthly fees uh ... to keep that park area going and to keep the services. Uh ... they really like to have swimming pools so forth so that they have a monthly fee for ... that would include, in addition to their purchase price. And I don't know if I mentioned the government backed uh ... uh ... mortgage program for people who want to buy uh ... a house in, in our area.

**Interviewer:** No, not yet. What is it?

**Mrs. Johnson:** It's called FHA (Federal Housing Authority) Chain Mortgage Program and the mortgage limit or the purchase price limit would be 100 in our area, would be 115,200. And they would require uh ... 3% down. And the mortgage uh ... interest rate over 30 years would be 7.5% on the balance for 30 years. So uh ... that would leave you with the mortgage of 113,760 which would include some uh ... private mortgage insurance to uh ... help the government from de ... defaulted mortgage in case people decided they couldn't, they were, they didn't want to pay their mortgage, then they had to pay this, this uh ... mortgage insurance. And so for that purchase of 115,200, the, with the 3% down, and that would be a principle on interest to 790 dollars a month and 35 dollars for um ... insurance. And then there would be taxes and additional real estate taxes on top of that. And actually then for that government backed loan of 115,200 for 3% down, you'd also have to have other cash for closing, so altogether you'd have to come to the closing table with 6,500 dollars for that mort, mortgage as opposed to 10,700 dollars for the 144,000 dollars purchase.

## Part Four Here's More

### Exercise One

1. OK … OK, this evening you're going to be traveling out on flight 317. Your seat is 17A, non-smoking, window.
2. A bag of frozen pea, two cartons of eggs, three eighty, please. Oh, no, should be three eighteen. Sorry for that.
3. Now, the weather forecast. Scotland and Northern Ireland will have heavy rain for much of the weekend and temperatures will drop to a cool sixty point six degrees Fahrenheit.
4. Hello, this is Doctor White's office. We are calling to remind you of your two fifty appointment for your annual checkup tomorrow.
5. The poll result shows just sixteen percent of the public gives the newspaper reporters very high ethical ratings. This percentage has decreased since 1981,when it was thirty percent.
6. The World Trade Center used to provide five hundred international corporations with the office space of four hundred and eighteen thousand six hundred square meters.
7. Last year our turnover went up by nearly a quarter, to seventy thousand pounds, and, if we take away the cost of renting the premises …
8. Someone told me you want to know the exact number of people in my country. That is one billion four hundred thirty-two million two hundred sixty-six thousand and forty-three.

### Exercise Two

**Conversation One Ordering Items from a Library**

**Librarian:** Good morning, City Central Library.

**Man:** Yes. I want to order some books and copies of articles please. You can send them to me through the post or courier, can't you?

**Librarian:** Yes, certainly. I'll just get the form and take down some details. First your name please, sir.

**Man:** Lester Mackie. That's capital M, A-C-K-I-E.

**Librarian:** Ok, Mr. Mackie. And your membership number…

**Man:** That's M9301274.

**Librarian:** M930 …

**Man:** 1274.

**Librarian:** Thank you. Now your address please. That's the address you want us to send the items to.

**Man:** It's 17 Westmead Road, Annandale.

**Librarian:** And could I have your phone number and your fax number please?

**Man:** Yes. The fax number is 863 9993.

**Librarian:** 863 9993.

**Man:** Correct. The daytime phone number is 02 579 6363 and after 5:00 p.m. it's 579 1857

**Librarian:** 579 1857. Thank you. And May I ask ...

**Conversation Two  Applying for the Telephone Banking Service**

**Clerk:** Hello. Can I help you?

**Customer:** Yes, I'd like to apply for your telephone banking service.

**Clerk:** OK. Could you fill in a form now?

**Customer:** Certainly.

**Clerk:** Right, could I have your full name, please?

**Customer:** Yes, it's John Peter Barnard.

**Clerk:** And your address, Mr. Barnard?

**Customer:** 24 Manor Road, Winchester.

**Clerk:** And the postcode?

**Customer:** SO23 9DY.

**Clerk:** Could I have your date of birth, please?

**Customer:** Yes, it's 31 October 1968.

**Clerk:** Thank you. And your daytime phone number?

**Customer:** 0131 6883 155.

**Clerk:** 0131 6883 155. And all I need now are your account details. Would you like the telephone banking just for your current account or for more than one account?

**Customer:** Just for my current account, please.

**Clerk:** OK. So, the sort code is 77 25 08 and could I have your account number, please?

**Customer:** 60877422.

**Clerk:** 60877422.

**Customer:** That's right.

**Clerk:** If you could sign the form here, Mr. Barnard, and then that's it. I'll register you and then we'll send you your information pack and membership card.

# Unit 4 Transportation and Traveling

## Part Two Listen Now

### Text One

**Interviewer:** Professor Bodman, how do you go to work every day, by car or by bus?

**Prof. Bodman:** Aah ... usually I go by car. In fact I go by car every day. It takes about four or five minutes unless there's a train crossing the highway. Sometimes then I have to wait for a couple of minutes. Aah ... it's about three or four miles from my house.

**Interviewer:** So you live very near where you work.

**Prof. Bodman:** Yes. I think some people here in Northfield would walk to work if they live close to downtown and some people would even bicycle to work. I have a colleague who does that. But most people would go by car.

**Interviewer:** So you live close to where you work, but you still prefer to go to work by car. How about the situation in other places?

**Prof. Bodman:** If you want to talk about how people in other places would go to work ... Let's say you live in a big city like New York City. Aah ... if you live inside the city, you will certainly go by public transportation, probably by subway.

**Interviewer:** Why is that?

**Prof. Bodman:** Because the subway system's very well developed and very quick, and also because to keep a car in a city will be very very expensive — to rent a special place for your car. On the other hand, if you live in the suburbs of New York City, you will probably take what's called a commuter train. These would be surface trains that also go very fast and have a, you know, service every hour, sometimes twice or three times an hour. Aah ... you can ride in on a commuter train, you can read your newspaper and sip a cup of coffee and get ready for the day's work, or you can of course use your mobile phone and talk to people.

**Interviewer:** So people in big cities don't usually go to work by car.

**Prof. Bodman:** Yes, most of them don't. Most people in a big city like New York or Chicago or San Francisco wouldn't dream of driving to work because of the congestion on the freeways and also because of the cost of parking downtown in New York. It might cost you 10 to 20 dollars to park for a day downtown New York whereas aah ... to get your round trip ticket on the commuter train would cost you much less than that.

**Interviewer:** Then how do people in a city like Minneapolis get to work? Do they drive or take bus or subway?

**Prof. Bodman:** Um ... in a medium sized city like Minneapolis, we don't have a well developed public transportation system and we don't have commuter rail yet. We're hoping to get commuter rail but that might take 5 to 10 years. So here most people do go to work by car. And we're in Northfield, aah ... which is about 40 miles from downtown. I would say a fair number of people from Northfield do drive. It takes about 45 minutes when traffic is good. But during high traffic time, during rush hours, it might take an hour; it might take an hour and half. So if you want to be smart, you'd probably leave Northfield at 5:30 a.m. and you could be downtown aah ... at 6:15. Then there will be no traffic whatsoever. If you wait, however, until 7:00 a.m., it might take you till 8:30 to get there.

## Text Two

**Interviewer:** I've heard that you've traveled a lot both in the States and in China. Would you please tell us how you usually travel ?

**Prof. Bodman:** Um ... I guess that depends on what kind of travel I'm doing. During the academic year, I will go to a couple of conferences. Aah ... that's usually by plane because our time's limited. We have like a three-day conference over weekends, so I will obviously fly. On the other hand, since I teach at college, I have a three-month summer vacation, all of June, all of July and all of August. So that gives me the freedom to travel more slowly in the summer and actually I prefer that.

**Interviewer:** So you don't like to travel in a hurry.

**Prof. Bodman:** I don't. So if I want to visit, for example, my sister in South Dakota — she lives about 900 miles from here, I could drive my car out. It would be a very nice two days' drive-out, another two days back. And the car allows you to do a lot of exploring along the way.

**Interviewer:** And plenty of time to enjoy the scenery along the roadsides.

**Prof. Bodman:** Yes. Um ... so either by plane or by car, I would say. Now I think that's true for most Americans, too. Aah ... most Americans would prefer to travel either by car or by plane, because both airplane travel and automobile travel is fairly highly developed. We have a national system of superhighways, which was, which started to be built in 1950s and 60s and was probably completed sometime in the late 1960s.

**Interviewer:** More than 30 years ago.

**Prof. Bodman:** Yes, more than 30 years ago. And that meant you can drive from New York to San Francisco or from New York to Seattle in under three days, if you drive almost continuously. Aah ... in many places you can drive 70 miles an hour. That's well over 120 kilometers an hour. Um ... on the other hand, we don't usually take the train because most of our trains now are freight trains, and much fewer passenger trains. If I want to go by passenger train, from, for example, Minneapolis to Chicago, there's only one train a day. Now if you have plenty of time, this is a great way to take a vacation and it saves driving and is more comfortable.

**Interviewer:** Is it cheaper than ...?

**Prof. Bodman:** No, it's not going to be much cheaper than the bus or the airplane. And the reason for that is aah ... if you travel by train, you probably want to eat at least one meal on the train, and that will cost you, you know, 10 dollars, let's say. If you want to sleep on the train and if you want to sleep in a compartment, that will cost you a lot more. So I think the train is a good thing for families who're going on vacation. Aah ... but otherwise it's not very useful for business people.

**Interviewer:** Then, which is the cheapest form of transportation?

**Prof. Bodman:** Bus travel is, aah ... tends to be the cheapest form of transportation. I think people who don't have cars and young people like students frequently travel by bus. Um ... I don't travel by bus because I've got a car and also because sitting in a bus you tend to get very cramped. It's like sitting in a tight airplane seat. And if you are taking a day-long trip, you'll be very stiff by the time you get out. And also sometimes the bus stops are in pretty part of the city, they aren't very lovely. So for these reasons I prefer to travel by car or by plane. But I know a lot of students and a lot of foreign visitors to the United States like to travel by long distance bus, Greyhound Lines, aah ... because there're some special promotions and some special inexpensive tickets for foreign visitors.

## III. Listen and choose the best answer to each question you hear.

1. How does Prof. Bodman go to conferences?
2. Why does he like to go to visit his sister by car?
3. How many days does it take to go by car from the East to the West in USA if you drive almost continuously?
4. Which of the following is the most expensive?
5. Why doesn't Prof. Bodman like to travel by bus?

# Part Four Here's More

## Exercise

### Paragraph One

Most large cities have some form of public transportation or transit, such as bus lines, subways, or commuter trains. For instance, in New York City and the suburbs of Washington, D.C., many people take commuter trains and subway trains (underground trains) from the outlying regions into the city to work during the day, then return on the train in the evening. There is often parking at the station in the outlying city or town, and people will go to their car from the train station and drive home. All major cities have some form of bus transportation. Typically, these routes will be differentiated by color code (such as a "blue" or "green" route, for example) and by route numbers. A "blue 10" route may be different from a "green 10" route. It is important to check a bus schedule that will tell you the times that the buses come to the terminals or to the bus stops (small covered benches at the side of the street along the route). Many buses will stop at a bus stop every ten or fifteen minutes, but they may be going different routes, which is why checking the number (and color) is important. Soon you will be able to memorize a route and schedule that you use frequently, and will know that the 8:10 a.m. blue bus with the number 15 is the one that goes near your work.

### Paragraph Two

You may choose to carpool to work with others. In carpools, people take turns driving, and usually several people go in one automobile to save on gas (and to cut down on pollution). One advantage of carpooling in some large cities is that there are special carpool lanes that you can use when driving if there are two or more passengers in the car. These lanes often move more quickly than the normal lanes during rush hours.

### Paragraph Three

Some people travel by airplane for business reasons: for instance, if an important business meeting or conference is in another state, then your business may pay for you to fly there. Often your work will make the arrangements. If you are flying for private reasons, you can contact an airline agency directly, or a local travel agent to help with making a reservation. Normally once reservations are made, they cannot be changed without paying a fee or a percent of the original fare. Sometimes certain days of the week and/or certain times of the day will have lower fares than others, so be sure to compare rates for different flights to the same destination. Prices may also vary between airlines. And normally the further ahead a flight is booked, the cheaper it is. Increasing security at airports has been a topic in recent news, and if you choose to fly, you will need to have your luggage and carry bags x-rayed and checked before traveling at security points near the entrances to departure gates.

# Unit 5

# Transportation and Traveling (Continued)

## Part Two Listen Now

### Text One

**Interviewer:** And how is traveling in the States different from that in China?

**Prof. Bodman:** I think there're two ways in which it's different. Um ... perhaps the first way is um ... similar to what I just said that people travel a lot more by car and by plane, not much by train. I know in China probably the train is still the favorite way to travel because it is really relatively reasonable. Airplane travel in China I would say is cheaper than travel in the United States, and yet for a Chinese income it's still quite expensive.

**Interviewer:** So that's one way in which things are different.

**Prof. Bodman:** Yes. Another way in which things are different is that at least in America if you're going to travel by plane, aah ... let's say from Minneapolis to New York, um ... the price let's say would be around 200 dollars. But the price also depends upon when you make your reservation. If you make your reservation two months in advance, it will probably be much cheaper than if you make it one week in advance.

**Interviewer:** So the earlier you book your ticket, the cheaper it is.

**Prof. Bodman:** Generally speaking, it's the case. In fact the difference in those prices could be very high. Um ... another difference is that the price of the ticket depends not upon the distance traveled but upon how many people like to travel a particular route. I just said that Minneapolis to New York is probably what I would consider a relatively inexpensive ticket and that's because there's lots of competition to get to New York. On the other hand, if you want to fly from Minneapolis to a small town where my sister lives, Rapid City, South Dakota, there's really only one major airline that serves that city and hence they have a monopoly and their price to go to Rapid City is almost as high as their price to go to New York from Minneapolis.

**Interviewer:** So the competition also decides the price of the ticket.

**Prof. Bodman:** Ya, I think you would find that surprising and maybe a little bit shocking, um ...

### Text Two

**Interviewer:** OK, now let's come back to traveling in USA. American people travel a lot. Can you tell us why they travel, and where they usually go within the States?

**Prof. Bodman:** Sure. Again this depends upon who you are. Aah ... business travelers would normally be traveling during the week. Aah ... and actually fares for traveling during the week are much higher than fares for traveling during the weekend. So leisure travel tends to be cheaper than business travel.

**Interviewer:** Is this because leisure travel often happens during the weekend?

**Prof. Bodman:** Yes, in a way, it is true. Let's talk primarily about leisure travel now, since that's something I know more about. Um ... I think it depends upon how old you are and it depends upon how much time you have. Let's say for example, aah ... you have a long weekend, a three-day holiday. Americans would have that over Labor Day and let's say July 4, Independence Day, aah ... maybe a couple of other times like Easter. On a three-day holiday, I think a lot of people would travel by car to see relatives who live nearby, to visit grandma or grandpa for example.

**Interviewer:** So leisure travels often go on during weekends and public holidays.

**Prof. Bodman:** Yes. On the other hand, most working people also have a paid vacation in a year which is usually a minimum of two weeks. Now if you've worked for a company longer, you might have three weeks, or even four weeks. But two weeks is the most common.

**Interviewer:** So how do people usually spend their two-week vacation?

**Prof. Bodman:** For the two-week vacation, again it would make sense in many cases to travel by car. You might want to go to a nearby resort where you could fish and boat, and swim. Or you might go, aah ... want to go camping in the mountains or in the forest, something like that.

**Interviewer:** I think people also fly to their holiday places.

**Prof. Bodman:** Yes. On the other hand, aah ... there are some farther away destinations where you would probably want to fly and when you've got there, then you might rent a car. Um ... if you are a child, let's say 12 years old, during the summer, your parents might send you to a summer camp. I know China now has summer camps, too. So this shouldn't be too strange. The summer camps are frequently run by organizations such as the boy scouts or the girl scouts. This is an opportunity for children to spend a week in the country and to learn how to swim or to use a sail boat or to survive in the wilderness, you know, build fires, live in tents and so forth.

**Interviewer:** That sounds really interesting for a child.

**Prof. Bodman:** Yes, it is interesting. If you're a college student, you'd also be doing some traveling. For holidays at Christmas, you'll probably fly home. At Thanksgiving, some students will also fly home for the holiday. And Spring Break seems to be a special tradition amongst college students. Normally you will have a week, maybe even ten days. So many college students, at least in the northern part of America, will club together, rent a car or use somebody's car and drive all the way to Florida to sit on the beach and drink beer and dance. Aah ... and so that can be relatively inexpensive.

**Interviewer:** It's cheap because they share the traveling expense.

**Prof. Bodman:** Right. If you're someone like me, a college teacher who has a long vacation in the summer, then um ... there're many different kinds of travel. Aah ... last summer my wife and I went on what you might call a kind of educational travel. We went to Ithaca, New York. That's where I did my graduate study. And we spent a week at what they call a Cornell Alumni University, where we both took a course for five days on how to design your own garden. This is a kind of travel aah ... that earns money for the college that you went to and earns money for college professors who want to work a little bit in the summer. And it's a different kind of vacation for people in which they feel they're not only seeing a new place but they're also learning something. So educational travel is um ... an interesting feature of travel in the United States.

**Interviewer:** And it sounds beneficial to all the people involved.

**Prof. Bodman:** It really is. Um ... many universities also organize travel overseas for their alumni. And I remember in 1991 I think, I went with my father who was, eh, around 80. We took a trip to New Zealand that was sponsored by Cornell University. And the university President traveled with us as well as a professor of biology. We had a very interesting holiday.

**Interviewer:** So your father was very healthy even at the age around 80.

**Prof. Bodman:** I believe so. I think probably the people who travel least are older people. But aah ... if you're a retired person, let's say 60 or so, one very common pattern is for you to spend aah ... winter aah ... traveling south, to a warmer location. Here in Minne ... in Minnesota where I live, aah ... the winters are fairly cold, somewhat like Harbin in winter in China. And so many retired people will go to either Arizona or Florida for the two coldest months. And then in the summer they will come back here and find it much cooler than down south. There're even some older or retired people who buy what's called an RV, a recreational vehicle which is like a miniature home on wheels. You have a bedroom, you have a tiny bathroom, you have a tiny kitchen.

**Interviewer:** I've seen it. It's usually well equipped.

**Prof. Bodman:** Aah, you can drive it . And it's sort of like your own little hotel that you can take with you. And they might travel for example all summer or some people even travel all the year. And this is one way in which you can visit your children or your grandchildren. So I think travel is a very interesting topic to talk about.

**IV. Listen and choose the best answer to each question you hear.**

1. When does the plane fare tend to be cheaper?
2. At least how long does a paid vacation last?
3. When people go to a nearby resort, what DON'T they usually do?
4. Who will go to a summer camp?
5. How do college students usually go to Florida at Spring Break?
6. What is an educational travel?
7. What kind of people would go south to escape the coldest months in Minnesota?
8. What is a recreational vehicle like?

## Part Four Here's More

### Exercise

**1. Martin Luther King Day**

Martin Luther King Day was the first new public holiday to be implemented in the USA since 1948 and actually came into effect in 1986. There were no special celebrations or ceremonies, but the holiday was an opportunity for the media to remind people of how Martin Luther King struggled to reshape the attitudes of Americans towards black people and in the end, how he paid the ultimate sacrifice for being prepared to speak out on the issue. Schools also use the commemoration as a focus to teach children about the history of slavery and prejudice, and the life and work of this great man.

**2. President's Day**

The origins of this holiday in February are that the birthdays of George Washington and Abraham Lincoln were on the 22nd and 12th February respectively. With Washington being the first president of the USA and Lincoln the president at the time of the Civil War, they had been singled out for holidays to commemorate their birth.

In 1971, however, President Richard Nixon decided that the two separate holidays should be discontinued and replaced by a one-day holiday in February called President's Day to celebrate not only the birthdays of Washington and Lincoln, but all US presidents through history.

**3. Memorial Day**

One of the oldest public holidays, Memorial Day is held to commemorate those who lost their lives fighting in the American Civil War. Initially called Declaration Day, the main remembrance ceremony takes place in the city of Waterloo in New York.

**4. Labor Day**

Labor Day is a public holiday dedicated to the social and economic achievements of US workers. It was proposed in 1882 in New York by the Central Labor Union and has been celebrated annually ever since.

**5. Columbus Day**

Rather more controversial is the celebration of the discovery of a group of islands off the coast of America in 1492 by one Christopher Columbus, which some say, led to the European colonization of the Americas.

Suffice to say, many native Americans (Indian Tribes) are not too pleased about the fact that the American nation sees fit to celebrate some European mercenary with a bad sense of direction claiming to have discovered a continent which their ancestors had been living on for thousands of years.

**6. Veterans Day**

Veterans Day is held in honor of those Americans who lost their lives fighting for their country. In 1921 an unknown American soldier who died in the First World War was buried in Arlington National Cemetery. This site, on a hillside overlooking the Potomac River and the city of Washington, became the focal point of reverence for American's veterans. Similar ceremonies occurred earlier in England and France, where an unknown soldier was buried in each nation's highest place of honor: in England, Westminster Abbey, and in France, the Arc de Triomphe. These ceremonies all took place on November 11th, giving universal recognition to the celebrated ending of World War I fighting at 11.00 am, 11th November, 1918, the day which became known as Armistice Day.

Armistice Day officially received its name in America in 1926 by a resolution of Congress and became a national holiday 12 years later.

In 1954, Congress was requested to make this day an occasion to honor all those who had served America in all wars, recognizing that peace was equally preserved by those who fought in World War II. President Eisenhower signed the bill proclaiming November 11th as Veterans Day.

The Focal point for official national ceremonies on Veterans Day continues to be at the Tomb of the Unknowns at Arlington Cemetery. At 11.00 a.m. on November 11th, a combined color guard representing all military services executes Present Arms at the tomb. A Presidential wreath is laid and a bugler plays.

# Unit 6

## Marriage and Family

**Part Two Listen Now**

### Text One

**Interviewer:** Professor Leming, I understand that you're teaching a course on marriage and family. The issues discussed in your class are very interesting. Would you please first say something about at what age American young people begin to date?

**Prof. Leming:** Well, I probably should say first what dating means in America. Aha ... in some ways, aah ... the traditional sense of dating means for a young man and a young woman to go somewhere together and have some kind of awareness that they're together and that the relationship they have right now is something other than just friends, that they're really interested in each other as a person of the opposite sex.

**Interviewer:** But what does dating mean in the modern sense?

**Prof. Leming:** More recently, dating has become, has changed to some extent, and groups of boys and groups of girls go together and they, as my, my children say they "hang out" together. And when they hang out together, it may be three boys and three girls or two boys and two girls, or maybe sometimes even different numbers of boys or girls. But over time, one boy gravitates towards one girl or vice versa. And so they begin to spend some exclusive time together. Out of that, then they might want just to be alone together and then they would call that a date.

**Interviewer:** So from hanging out together with lots of boys and girls to spending some exclusive time with one girl or one boy, it takes time.

**Prof. Leming:** Absolutely. And my own children, aah ... they used to have this phrase, aah ... "going together." And "going together" means that they're a couple. When my son was in elementary school, aah ... maybe he was ten or eleven or twelve, he had a girl that would call him on the phone. And, and they would call every night and they would talk to each other on the phone. They didn't go anywhere and they didn't go out on a date, but they used to say, "We're going out." And "we're going out" means "we're a couple." And they would talk to each other, but they didn't go anywhere. And I used to say to my son, "You're going out. Where're you going?" He says, "No, we're just going out," which meant they basically, they were a couple.

**Interviewer:** They seem to start with a telephone dating.

**Prof. Leming:** Yes. Then when they got older, they would begin to date someone steady. Then they would say, "We're going together" or "We're going out." And they really would go out. So, aah ... then, then the persons become like "a couple." When that starts, usually 16, 17, 18 years old in America. And the reason for that time is because young people then are able to drive. And they drive their parents' car or they get a job and they try to buy their own car. So in American society, to date basically means to have independence and to be able to go some place. And it usually means to go out in a car. So I would say most young people start dating when they're like 16, 17, 18 years old. And that's pretty normal.

**Interviewer:** OK. Whether you can drive or not decides whether you can go out to date with your boy- or girlfriend. And how do young people select their spouses?

**Prof. Leming:** Well, once they start dating, aah ... I think that, that you wouldn't want to underestimate the power of a kind of sexual attraction that a boy has for a girl or a girl has for a boy. That's very important for couples. But they tend to select people or they tend to be attracted to people who're pretty similar to themselves. And they meet these people aah ... they meet typically in school or in their recreational hobbies or in places where people have a like interest. They can meet them in church, they can meet them in school, they can meet them in, in, at a baseball field or something that they might want to do in general. So they would select them. When they finally select someone, they usually like to find people who're of similar age, of similar racial background. Aah ... African-Americans tend to marry African-Americans, and Caucasians marry Caucasians, and Asian-Americans tend to marry Asian-Americans.

**Interviewer:** So they select someone of their same ...

**Prof. Leming:** Yes, their same social circumstances, people of similar kinds of money and education, and religious background. Those kinds of ... they look for those kinds of similarities. And they're attracted to people like that.

## Text Two

**Interviewer:** To get married, what are the bride and groom required to possess legally and individually?

**Prof. Leming:** From a legal point, they must get a marriage license. And the marriages in the United States are not governed by the national authorities; they're governed by the local state or in your area province. So aah ... they would aah ... they would have to go to aah ... a state agency and in American society, we have, we have the national government, we have the state government and then there's a smaller unit called county government. And they go to the county to get marriage license.

**Interviewer:** So the marriage license is issued by the county government.

**Prof. Leming:** Yes. The county requires that the people are free to marry, so they have to make sure that the person who wants to marry the other person is not already married. You only allow one marriage partner in the United States, not more than one. Secondly they have to be sure that they don't have any disease. And so they, they have to take blood test to make sure they don't have syphilis or they don't have AIDS, something like that.

**Interviewer:** So these are the two requirements the couple must meet if they want to get married.

**Prof. Leming:** You are right. And then after they, they fill out the marriage license form, then they have to go before someone who has the authority by the state to marry them.

**Interviewer:** Who exactly?

**Prof. Leming:** In American society, it is usually a minister of a church or some kind of a religious leader. It can be a judge, it can be a aah ... Justice of the Peace, it can be a number of other people who have, who have authority to marry. Once they have been married, there's a kind of ceremony. Then they take their marriage license and register at the county. And then, then once it's done, from then on they're married.

**Interviewer:** And it's a legal marriage.

**Prof. Leming:** Ya. Now it is also required by the state that the couple at some point of time have sexual intercourse because if a couple were, aah...married and they never had sexual intercourse, and one person wanted to end the relationship, the state could say there never was an original marriage. But if once that's taken place and it's a legal marriage, then the only thing that can end the marriage is a divorce which is pretty, is not that difficult to obtain even though it is difficult for the people emotionally, or a death.

**Interviewer:** So it's easy to get divorced so far as formalities are concerned.

**Prof. Leming:** That's true.

**Interviewer:** Just now you mentioned the marriage ceremony. Well, could you say something about it?

**Prof. Leming:** Americans like marriages and we make big things out of marriages. On average, on average, aah ... Americans spend almost 20,000 dollars for a typical wedding for everything. So the exchange rate now is 7 to 1. Is that right? RMB to American dollars?

**Interviewer:** About 8 to 1.

**Prof. Leming:** So that'll be 160,000 yuan. Very expensive. We make ... now you can do it much cheaper. My son was married two years ago. And I think they spent about 2,000 dollars. What they did was they, they had aah ... a very simple wedding and they went to some place for a reception, then they had some food and you know they didn't make too expensive.

**Interviewer:** Was it typical?

**Prof. Leming:** I don't think so. Some couples make big things, sit-down meal, a meal before they have the practice of the wedding. They give lots of gifts. It can be very expensive. So couples like to save their money to make sure that they have enough money for a nice wedding. Now typically the parents of the, if it's a younger couple, the parents of the bride and the parents of the groom will help or pay for that.

**Interviewer:** That sounds like Chinese parents.

**Prof. Leming:** And in American society, the parents of the bride pay more than the parents of the groom. But things're changing in American society. Today couples are getting married older and older. So I think a typical age for men and women in America to get married is somewhere in the neighborhood of 26 to 28 years of age.

**Interviewer:** After getting married, people will have children. In raising children, what do American parents emphasize?

**Prof. Leming:** The most important thing that American parents emphasize is independence. We like our children to grow up and become self-reliant and independent. And they would not depend on their parents or their grandparents or other members of the family to support them.

**Interviewer:** So you encourage financial independence.

**Prof. Leming:** Yes, we encourage resourcefulness, and people will be able to be self-reliant. We encourage aah ... them to think for themselves. And so our children often aah ... will aah ... even stand up to their parents and disagree with their parents. And in some ways the parents are responsible for that because they want their children to be independent. And as a result, they get this, they get kids to talk back. I think when I've been in China, it seems Chinese and other Asian people that I've known in Japan, in Thailand, where I go often, that the children seem to be more obedient to their parents.

**Interviewer:** Yes, obedience to parents or teachers is regarded as a kind of virtue in China, where I'm from.

**Prof. Leming:** In American society, obedience's important, but independence in some ways is encouraged. And so sometimes children are disobedient to their parents. We teach our children to respect their parents, but we want them to think for themselves, especially as they get older.

**Interviewer:** OK. Thank you very much.

**Prof. Leming:** You are welcome.

## Part Four Here's More

### Exercise One

**Marriage**

Marriages are not "arranged" in the United States. Young people are expected to find a husband or wife on their own; their parents do not usually help them. In fact, parents are frequently not told of marriage plans until the couple has decided to marry. This means that parents have little control, and generally not much influence, over whom their children marry. Americans believe that young people should fall in love and then decide to marry someone they can live happily with, again an evidence of the importance of an individual's happiness. Of course, in reality this does not always happen, but it remains the ideal, and it shapes the views of courtship and marriage among young Americans.

Over the years, the value placed on marriage itself is determined largely by how happy the husband and wife make each other. Happiness is primarily on companionship. The majority of American women value companionship as the most important part of marriage. Other values, such as having economic support and the opportunity to have children, are seen by many as less important.

### Exercise Two

**Marriage and Wedding Customs**

There are many customs and traditions surrounding marriage and particularly around the wedding activities themselves. Once again, it is very hard to generalize about these customs, as they vary so much among different people, but there are some customs that are quite generally observed. It is no longer necessary for a young man to ask permission of a girl's father for her "hand," but most young people very much want their parents' approval of the person they hope to marry. It is still traditional for a young man to give his fiancée a diamond ring at the beginning of their engagement period. As for the actual wedding ceremony and related celebrations, traditionally it is the bride's family who pays for these expenses. The wedding ceremony can be a very simple one, with only a few family members and close friends present, or it can be very elaborate, with hundreds of people in attendance. The traditional reception that follows the ceremony can be as simple as cookies and punch in the church or as elaborate as a large sit-down dinner held at a local hotel with a dance with a private orchestra following the dinner. Sometimes people are invited only to the wedding or only to the reception. At any rate, these events can usually be attended only by invitation. Wedding gifts are expected from people who receive wedding invitations. Occasionally people choose not to have any kind of religious service at their wedding and opt to get married in a civil ceremony in a government building. However, a civil ceremony is not necessary if a couple decides to get married in a religious ceremony. Priests, ministers, and rabbis are legally empowered to marry couples, and it is not necessary to have both a civil and religious ceremony. By the way, there's an interesting tradition associated with weddings that is rather hard to explain, but then many traditions are. It is said every bride at her wedding should be wearing or carrying "something old, something new, something borrowed, something blue." The bride will be checked at the last minute to be sure that she has one of each of these. There are some other customs similar to this one that are rather superstitious in nature. For example, people believe that it is bad luck for the groom to see the bride in her wedding dress before the ceremony. And immediately following the ceremony, as the couple leave the church, people at the ceremony will throw rice at them to signal fertility — that is, a hope that they will have many children.

# Unit 7 Divorce

## Part Two Listen Now

### Text One

**Interviewer:** So Michelle I know that you're studying for a doctoral degree and also you're teaching a course, Family and Marriage. And would you please tell us something about the divorce rate in the United States?

**Michelle:** OK. Uh ... the divorce rate in the United States is uh ... the highest in, among uh ... industrialized nations in the world. But it's very difficult to measure. Um ... the way social scientists do it is to take the number of divorces per one thousand married women. Um ... and, currently in the United States, that rate is somewhere between 20 and 25. So the divorce rate in the United States is about 22 divorces per one thousand married women. A lot of times we hear about the divorce rate being 50%. And how terrible and tragic this is that the United States has a divorce rate of 50%! And this is a difficult thing to measure as well. When we talk about the divorce rate being 50%, uh ... we are not talking about the fact that there might be, say in 1999, two million marriages and one million divorces, which are accurate numbers. Uh ... that's not what 50% means.

**Interviewer:** Then what does it mean?

**Michelle:** The 50% means that among all the people getting married this year in 1999 for example, 50% of them throughout the course of their lifetime will divorce. So it's a prediction. It's not a reflection of this years' status. It's a longitudinal uh ... prediction of what the divorce rate will be amongst the people who get married in any given year.

**Interviewer:** I see.

**Michelle:** But if we just take the number of people who get divorced currently in any given year, it's the number of divorces for per one thousand married women, and that number is right around uh ... 20 to 25. And since the mid 1980s, that number has maintained a pretty steady rate. In fact it's decreased to some extent, so somewhere between 20 and 21, and 22 up to 25 in the mid 80s, and back down to 22 or 21 now. Uh ... the divorce rate is not increasing right now in the United States.

**Interviewer:** What do you think are the common factors that cause a marriage to break up?

**Michelle:** Um ... that's a difficult question to answer because everyone will look at their own situation. Uh ... and say, uh ... you know, I got divorced because um ... my husband was an alcoholic or because uh ... we had communication problems or because I was just unhappy. And all of these are very, seem like very individualistic uh ... reasons for divorcing.

**Interviewer:** So people get divorced for different reasons, all very individualistic.

**Michelle:** Yes. But I think if we look at the whole picture, uh ... sociologically speaking, uh ... we can take these individual stories, you know, if there's abuse, if there's alcoholism, if there's communication problems ... whatever the reasons might be, and look at it from an American sociological point of view, what we see is an increasing emphasis placed on individualism, uh ... a lack of emphasis placed on community and family involvement in your marriage. Uh ... so you know, 150 years ago, in the, even in the United States you had a lot more influence from your parents and other family members in the community about whom you marry. And you got married for very practical reasons. Economically women needed someone to provide for them; men needed to marry somebody who could provide children and nurturing, and domestic service.

**Interviewer:** That's not true any more.

**Michelle:** Ya, when I got married, I didn't need to get married for financial reasons because I have a separate career of my own and have financial independence from my husband. So today we have an increased emphasis on emotions. And you marry somebody because you are in love with them. And you find you're a soul mate and it's all very nice and on the back of the Hallmark greeting card. Uh ... and so of course what happens is, the more emphasis you place on having only one other person meet every single one of your emotional needs which by the way is impossible, the more likely you are to become disappointed. And you place that one on top of the fact that it's easy to get a divorce in this country.

**Interviewer:** So you mean it's more difficult to meet the emotional needs than financial ones.

**Michelle:** It's doubtless. Especially since 1973, with the No-Fault Divorce Law, you take all these things in consideration. Uh ... societally speaking, it helps explain why people are more likely to get divorced than they used to be.

## Text Two

**Interviewer:** What do you think people consider a woman who has got divorced? People think it's a bad thing or a good thing?

**Michelle:** Uh ... first of all I think it makes a difference if you're asking about a woman or a man because I think there's a difference in how people view women and men, uh ... divorced or not divorced. Uh ... there's definitely less stigma or negative labeling on people who have been divorced in this country. Uh ... recently in my Sociology of Marriage and Family class, I asked students how many of them in some way have been affected by divorce, whether it's a friend or parents or parents of friends', uh ... and 75% of them raised their hand. If I would have asked this question 50 years ago, maybe 3 or 4 would raise their hand, and they would be very shy about it because there was a lot of negative stereotypes involved with being divorced.

**Interviewer:** How has it changed?

**Michelle:** It's kind of like a cycle. And I don't know which comes first, uh ... the acceptance or the numbers, but the more people you have doing something, the more acceptable it seems because the standards and the norms change. So the more divorces there are, the easier it is to say I'm divorced and not feel like somebody is going to stereotype you negatively or view you as a failure.

**Interviewer:** So no negative feelings on those who got divorced at all?

**Michelle:** Of course, those feelings still exist. I have a brother who's going through divorce right now, and he's very worried about what his friends think about him, and most worried about what his kids think about all of the things that are going on. So you know having said that, you know, there was a lot of stigma attached to it in the past, you have to recognize there is still a stigma today. And it's not that people go into the divorce situations very lightly.

**Interviewer:** I see.

**Michelle:** Some people do of course. And I mean there are people who married five or six times and then got divorced a lot. You used to start to wonder what they think. But there's still, there's still negative stereotyping and worries about what people think about you. It's just a little bit less than what used to be.

**Interviewer:** OK. Do you think the divorce rate in USA keeps increasing or decreasing?

**Michelle:** Uh ... you mean in the 20th century or in the 1990s?

**Interviewer:** In recent years.

**Michelle:** In recent years, it's been uh ... well, you had a vast increase uh ... like I said in 1973 when the No-Fault Divorce Law was passed, and it steadily increased since then as more and more women gained economic independence from men and men's earnings declined as well. Mid 80s, you saw uh ... the peak, the highest point, uh ... of, of the divorce rate. And since the mid 1980s it has maintained about the same. It has not really gone up that much. It's ... in fact, it's maybe decreased.

## Part Four Here's More

### Exercise One

1. And you have always taught the first grade?
2. So you feel tired. Anything else? Do you ever lose your temper?

3. And what do you do, personally, to deal with the stress of your job?
4. OK, well, I wanted to ask you, what do you think is the best age, the best period in life?
5. Well, what I wanted to ask you about first is what differences have you seen, um, between the ways girls perform, and the ways boys perform at various ages?
6. Communicate that way. Huh, so you say your parents didn't hug or kiss him. Did they hug or kiss you? I mean, within your family, do, in Japan do people hug each other? Like, did your mother hug you?
7. Are there any difference in eye contact that you've noticed between Japanese and Americans?
8. Let's talk some more about your courses at the college. Do you remember any study projects that you were involved in?
9. And finally, what advice or words of warning would you give to school leavers considering a career in this country?
10. Um, one last question. What about your future? Have you any immediate plans?

## Exercise Two

**Excerpt One**

**Sue:** Then tell me, what is your main responsibility during a flight?

**Julie:** That's hard to say really. Well, we're responsible for all the needs and demands of each and every passenger, for up to 10 hours on some long haul flights. Not to mention the safety of the plane and all the passengers. I suppose, if I have to come up with a single answer, it'd be passenger comfort.

**Excerpt Two**

**Sue:** And finally, what advice or words of warning would you give to school leavers considering a career in this country?

**Julie:** That's a difficult question. Let me think ... I'd say think long and hard about why you want to do it. It's not all glamorous, and it can be very hard work. It affects your family and your social life. I mean, I don't have any social life to speak of, unless it's with my colleagues at the airline. But, all the same, it remains a rewarding and challenging career. You certainly never get bored.

# Unit 8 Divorce (Continued)

## Part Two Listen Now

### Text One

**Michelle:** So instead of 24 divorces per one thousand married women now, it's 22 divorces. So you know, it's not that big of a decrease, but it is decreasing uh ... and at the very least it is staying about the same and not increasing.

**Interviewer:** How does this happen?

**Michelle:** Uh ... I don't know. And I, I think that this is something that a lot of researchers are just now beginning to understand. But my guess is that if you have um ... a very high divorce rate, the highest ever, say in mid 80s, maybe now we have something like a backlash where you have people see the high divorce rate and they get scared. They say, you know, because of our divorce rate the American marriage is falling apart or it's in decline. And then they do the opposite to try to maintain marriage as much as possible. So maybe we have reached the highest point, we're saying, you know, we have to do something to try to combat the problem. And maybe the numbers are reflecting a little bit that idea.

**Interviewer:** Any other possible reasons?

**Michelle:** Another possible reason might be just that uh ... you know fewer people are getting married than before and people are waiting longer. So divorce might become uh ... an interesting concept when you look at just the number of people who even get married.

**Interviewer:** What do you think are the factors that influence the marriage? I mean what do you think are the factors that can keep a marriage working or maintain a marriage?

**Michelle:** Hum. Well, I'm not sure you're asking the right person, but, because I'm not a marriage and family therapist, as a sociologist, I look at the things from a structural point of view. Uh ... I think in order to keep a marriage working, the first step — this is why I teach this — is to realize that we live in an individualistic society. And to say, OK, if I'm unhappy in my marriage, will separating make me happy probably? Do I just need to think about myself? And especially when there are children involved, that are young or any age children, uh ... to reconsider the selfishness, I think, is very important.

**Interviewer:** So think twice before getting divorced and think about others instead of only you yourself.

**Michelle:** Ya. So if you're going through a difficult marriage, to reconsider how selfish you are being is an important question. Uh ... I'm thankful for divorce in some cases because there's no reason anybody should be in an abusive situation, and there's no reason that anybody should be in a situation that they find uncomfortable. So we need to have it.

**Interviewer:** Divorce is, in this sense, necessary.

**Michelle:** But if you're in a marriage where you're just unhappy and you can't figure out what's going on, evaluate your communication pattern. Um...are you being honest with your spouse? Do you trust your spouse? Uh... do you say things that are hurtful to your spouse? Or do you say things in front of your children or to your children that indicate you don't respect or trust your spouse?

**Interviewer:** So first consider whether it's your fault.

**Michelle:** Exactly. Uh ... there's, you know, there's a research done on domestic violence that says that the family has both the most intimate setting and the most violent setting. And so we're the closest with people that we can become the most angry with. And you have to keep that in mind. It's very easy to be uh ... critical of somebody else; it's very easy to be selfish and not give up things that you might really like. So if you really, really like to work, and you really like to stay at work until 7:30 p.m., uh ... and your wife says: "You know, it's really important for me to have a family dinner at 6:30," then you need to go into work an hour earlier. That would be my advice. Uh ... then you need to do things that evaluate your own uh ... situation. If you're uh ... being told by your spouse that you're too critical, evaluate how you communicate your feelings. If you're upset with somebody, are you presenting your opinion in a productive manner or are you just being critical of your spouse?

## Text Two

**Interviewer:** So communication pattern's very important.

**Michelle:** Yes. Um ... there's all sorts of statistics that I can give you about how long your engagement should be or how old you should be when you get married. Uh ... do you want me to give some of those?

**Interviewer:** Yes, please.

**Michelle:** Yeah, OK. Well, I can give some statistics that the, the uh ... if you marry somebody before you're 20 years old, uh ... you're more likely to get divorced. If you marry somebody less than six months after having met them, you're more likely to get divorced. If you marry somebody after you have been engaged for more than 3 years, you may be more likely to get divorced.

**Interviewer:** Why?

**Michelle:** Because that might show kind of a lack of commitment, a lack of saying "Yes, OK, I will settle down now and get married to you." Um ... if you have a history of a poor relationship with your parents or your siblings, uh ... you may not know how to deal with conflict or how to communicate effectively. So that might be a factor. Um ... if marriage patterns amongst your parents were very unstable, if your parents got divorced, you may be more likely to get divorced. But what actually more than likely happens is you're less than likely even to get married.

**Interviewer:** That makes sense.

**Michelle:** So instead of, instead of uh ... getting married in the first place and ending up in divorce, you might not even trust the institution of marriage at all because you see that in your parents — it didn't work. And so why would it work for me? Um ... some people say that if you have a very different socio-economic background from your partner, that might make some extra challenges also. Not saying this is a wrong thing, but if you look at couples that marry from different racial or ethnic backgrounds, there's an extra set of challenges that they have to overcome, that are from outside of them. Um ... there might be stereotypes or prejudices, or, you know, anything that might make their lives just difficult in general, that would add challenges to their marriage.

**Interviewer:** It would really do.

**Michelle:** Um ... if you live with somebody, uh ... cohabit as we say, um ... before you're married and while you're living together, you have no immediate plans to get married, uh ... you're more likely to get divorced. So, uh ... again that might show maybe a lack of commitment. Uh ... so those are, those are the things that come to mind, those individual reasons, communication problems, uh ... feelings of respect and intimacy, honesty and intimacy. Uh ... but those are also larger factors: how old you are, how your family situation is, and realizing what, if what you're doing is selfish or not.

## IV. Listen and answer the questions you hear.

1. Why are people more likely to get divorced if they marry somebody after they have been engaged for more than 3 years?
2. What does a history of a poor relationship with your parents or your siblings mean?
3. What might happen to those whose parents got divorced?
4. What might face those who marry from different racial or ethnic backgrounds?

# Part Four Here's More

## Exercise

1. **Interviewer:** Really? Is there something that the police department does to help you deal with this stress?

**Sam:** Yes, there are several programs that most police departments have in place. One is a physical training or exercise program — an established program where some part of your day is spent on some type of physical exercise. They've found that that's a great stress reducer. Um, there's also a psychological program with counseling for officers to help them reduce their stress. And there are several discussion groups. They've found that sometimes just sitting around and talking about the stress — with other officers — helps to reduce it. So, those things are available.

2. **Interviewer:** And what do you do, personally, to deal with the stress of your job?

**Sam:** Well, during the baseball season, I'm the biggest baseball fanatic, and I will either be reading about baseball, or listening to baseball, or watching baseball. Another thing I try to do is to get some sort of exercise every day. And then, I work hard at keeping my personal relationships, especially my relationship with my wife, at the peak. I'm very fortunate that I have a good relationship with my wife, and a good marriage. So when I come home, I can talk about my day with her, and then just forget about it.

3. **Interviewer:** Dennis, let me ask you a different question, and that is do you think that a child's economic and maybe social background makes a difference in school performance?

**Dennis:** Yeah, you know, there is a pattern. The elementary school where I had most of my teaching experience and where I eventually became principal, uh, was an interesting one because it sat between two very different parts, parts of, of this community. Uh, one part is a very wealthy neighborhood built around a world-class golf course. And then the other part of the community is low-income housing, including a complex of families, um, where the mother has just been released from the local women's prison. So, you know, I really saw a wide economic and social range, and, and I've seen low-income families that just do a great job of getting their kids to school and supporting them in their education. But, you know, I think the predictable cliché there is true — that those kids who are supported do better. Kids whose parents value education do better. And you know, another big economic issue is technology — access to computers at home in their bedroom — they just do better!

4. **Interviewer:** I believe there are other advantages as well?

**Dr. Clarke:** There are several. Every few days it covers the entire earth. So it produces large quantities of data. It measures the temperature from two angles, which allows correction for any effects that the intervening atmosphere may be having on its readings. Its field of view has a width of 500 km and it measures the temperature to 0.3 degree centigrade.

# Unit 9

# Teaching at High School and University

## Part Two Listen Now

### Text One

**Interviewer:** Uh, Professor Solid, you're from the department of Education. Uh ... can you tell us what qualifications one must have in order to be a schoolteacher or a college professor in the United States?

**Prof. Solid:** First let's talk about the schoolteachers here in the United states. To teach in a public school, one has to have a license or a certificate, a teaching certificate. To attain that, there are three things that must happen. It's ... the candidate must have a bachelor's degree with a defined teaching major, which is second. And finally you should complete and approve the Teaching Education Program. And the Teaching Education Program are courses and experiences of teaching. And the courses involve uh ... the professional part of it, how-to, why the learning theory, those kinds of thing. At the college level, the license of certificate is not required, but the terminal degree is. For example, I have Ph. D. and I'm teaching here at college because I have earned that and also a Master's degree.

**Interviewer:** So to teach in high schools, a teaching certificate is a must, while at college, a Ph. D. degree is necessary.

**Prof. Solid:** Yes, but there are exceptions. We have a person in our staff, for example, who has master plus 60 hours. He doesn't have a Ph. D., but he's still a valuable part of our program and we consider his qualification is high because he has so many years' of actual classroom teaching experience which we think is equally important for our work.

**Interviewer:** I see. But so far as the salary and other welfare are concerned, is there any difference between a schoolteacher and a college professor?

**Prof. Solid:** There isn't really uh ... lots of differences between uh ... a high school or junior high or an elementary school teacher or a college professor. Maybe in the long run, teaching at college or university, one can make a little but more money toward the end. But they have a higher, they have additional expenses because they're getting the higher degree. When you are teaching in the public schools, there is a pay scale. In it, they used to start out based upon non-experience, just bachelor's degree. And they earn hours of credits and as they gather years' of experience, the pay goes up likewise at college level. But at college level, your benefits in both cases. But all in all, uh ... my guess is that I would be working at about the same amount of money per year now had I stayed teaching high school as I do now as a college professor.

**Interviewer:** For most teachers and professors, why do you think they chose the teaching profession instead of other career which might offer them a higher salary?

**Prof. Solid:** Oh, that's a good question. Here in the United States, teachers and professors aren't paid that well, particularly teachers, and especially in the areas of mathematics, science and other areas where uh ... The paying industry and business in the high profession, like medicine and law, pay much much higher than for teaching. But there are people who are drawn and attracted to the profession of teaching. Generally these are people who are service-orientated, who like working with people, who aren't so concerned about making money. They just want comfortable living, but they enjoy working with people; they enjoy the active ... the system these people are learning and growing, and stretching. And these are the people that are attracted to this kind of work profession.

## Text Two

**Interviewer:** In your opinion, what are the factors that could possibly make a person be a good teacher?

**Prof. Solid:** A good teacher has to uh ... have everything in place in terms of uh ... what they want to do, how they see themselves, but more importantly how they see other people. I have a theory about this. It's not proven, but it's something that I've gained from my own experience. I think that there probably are four needs that must exist to someone who uh ... enjoy teaching, enjoy the life of being a teacher. One is they must enjoy the active teaching. That involves not only assisting the young learner in growing and stretching, and gathering information in developing skills, but it also involves assessment, evaluation, disciplining, uh ... management, uh ... giving grades, uh ... everything that has inherited the whole active teaching. And the person who wants to be a teacher needs to, need to uh ... needs to like that, be able to do that.

**Interviewer:** So first thing is one must love teaching.

**Prof. Solid:** Right. Also the teacher must uh ... like the content area. They must have a passion for the area that they are majoring in. Whether it's mathematics or biology, or chemistry, or history, or art, they must really enjoy that, so they grow themselves, so they can uh ... be enthusiastic and share that enthusiasm with the young learners, so they must like the active teaching, they must like the content.

**Interviewer:** They must love what they teach.

**Prof. Solid:** Ya. Thirdly they must like uh ... the uh ... they must also like young people. If it's the younger age that they are working with, they must like children and like being with them and helping them. If it's the older young person, they must like working at lessons and understand who they are and where they are. They must like young people.

**Interviewer:** So they must love their students.

**Prof. Solid:** Yes. Finally, fourth, they must like themselves. They must feel good about who they are and what they are doing. And they might ... they must be ... have some pride and be involved in the profession and share their profession with others. So I think those four things must exist. If one is missing, teaching is really hard work. It's a long day, you are not paid that well, but there are many other rewards that come for those who, who uh ... who have chosen to be teacher and enjoy themselves in their profession.

**Interviewer:** So, as I know, you have been a college professor for nearly 30 years and before that you were a school ... a high school teacher. What has challenged you most either as a schoolteacher or a college professor?

**Prof. Solid:** Oh, I think, yes, it is true. I taught the seventh, eighth grades in junior high. I taught high school Grades Nine, Ten, Eleven and Twelve. I taught two areas. I taught mathematics and also taught physics and science at the junior high and senior high level. And then secondly, I taught at college level and I've taught adults as well. At public school level, with the seventh, eighth, ninth, tenth, eleventh and twelfth grades, I think that probably one of the largest challenges for teachers is to attempt to meet the needs of the large diversity of their students within their classroom.

**Interviewer:** I can understand that. It's really difficult.

**Prof. Solid:** And certainly motivation is a challenge for teachers here in the United States. There are many students who're self-motivated, who are goal-orientated, who're focused. But as you know students in the United States uh ... It's free education. They're required to go and there are many students that come from backgrounds, who uh ..., where education doesn't seem to be very important.

**Interviewer:** So you need to motivate them.

**Prof. Solid:** Ya, somehow it's the teacher's job to motivate students to see the value in learning. And that's a challenge. But also there is such variety in not only the backgrounds of the students but also in learning styles. Different students learn differently, whether they are editorial or visual or concrete thinkers. And so that's a challenge, too, to try to meet the needs of all the students that they are working with. At college level, of course, I'm more specific here to college level when working with teacher candidates. These are uh ... young people generally at the ages of 20, 21 and 22, 23 who are preparing to become teachers. They're working towards the teaching license that I referred earlier.

**Interviewer:** So you're now training teachers.

**Prof. Solid:** Definitely. Many of these people, all of these people have just been involved in going through elementary school, and junior high and senior high, and one or two years college and because they've been involved in education or maybe their parents have been teachers themselves, many of them believe that they already know or at least know about how to teach. And they just want to get on with it. And so the challenge for us is to demonstrate to them that teaching is not only an art but it is also a science. There is a science to teaching. There is a research that shows that certain things do make uh ... teaching more effective, that there are things teachers can do to make learning uh ... more uh ... practical. And that's a challenge for us.

**Interviewer:** So different levels present different challenges. Thank you so much.

## III. Listen and choose the best answer to each question you hear.

1. What is Professor Solid's theory based on?
2. What DOESN'T the active teaching involve?
3. Which of the statements is true?
4. What must Professor Solid especially focus on when training teacher candidates?

## Part Four Here's More

## Exercise

### American Education System

The American education system requires that students complete 12 years of primary and secondary education prior to attending university or college. This may be accomplished either at public (or government-operated) schools, or at private schools. Most American children start school at the age of five. The first year at school is called kindergarten. All the children are required to enroll in the American education system. The second year at school is considered the first year of primary school and is referred to as first grade. Primary school most commonly consists of five years of education, referred to as first through fifth grade.

After the primary education, children will advance to secondary school. Secondary school most commonly consists of a total of seven years, referred to as sixth through twelfth grades. The ninth through twelfth grades are most commonly referred to as high school. Upon completion of twelfth grade, students are awarded a certificate called the high school diploma. In the American education system, students must have obtained a high school diploma before they are admitted into college or university.

Students who have completed high school and would like to attend college or university must attend what is referred to as an undergraduate school. These are schools that offer either a two-year degree (called an associate degree) or a four-year degree (called a bachelor's degree) in a specific course of study. That course of study is called the major. While most schools that offer a four-year degree will admit students who have not yet chosen a major, all students are required to select (or declare) a major by their second year at school. Students who complete an associate degree can continue their education at a four-year school and eventually complete a bachelor's degree.

Students with a bachelor's degree can continue their education by pursuing one of two types of degrees. The first is a master's degree. This is usually a two-year degree that is highly specialized in a specific field. Students are sometimes admitted to a master's degree program only if they have a bachelor's degree in a closely related field. However, there are many exceptions to this, such as with students who want to pursue a Master's in Business Administration (MBA) degree. Students who want to advance their education even further in a specific field can pursue a doctorate degree, also called a Ph.D. A Ph.D. degree can take between three and six years to complete, depending on the course of study chosen, the ability of the student, and the thesis that the student has selected. The thesis must be completed prior to earning the degree. It is always required of students pursuing a Ph.D., and may sometimes be required of students pursuing a master's degree (depending on the school).

## Unit 10 Campus Life

### Part Two Listen Now

### Text One

**Interviewer:** Rachel, you're a senior at St. Olaf College, aren't you?

**Rachel:** Yes. Uh ... I'm in my senior year here at St. Olaf College. Uh ... my, I come from a family in Wisconsin near Milwaukee and I'm studying Studio Art and Education.

**Interviewer:** Uh ... can you tell how many courses you are studying? And what are they?

**Rachel:** Well, this semester, I have four courses because it's the last semester uh ... at college.

I have one course where I work only in my senior project from Art classes using photography. I have um ... Art History class; I take a linguistic course and also uh ... a Figure and Drawing class. So that's four courses and twelve times a week I have class.

**Interviewer:** OK. So what do you and other students do after class?

**Rachel:** Oh, there are lots of things to do after class. After class, uh ... I'm usually back to my dorm and talk to my roommates and meet some friends. We might go out for a coffee or go for sports. Uh ... there're teams that we can join, play volleyball or baseball. You know, that's a big sport. Uh ... the weather's nice here. In winter, uh ... we might go skiing or sleighing.

**Interviewer:** Do many students do part-time jobs and what kind of jobs they usually find?

**Rachel:** Um ... I think this is one of the difficult things for collegians to balance your work time, your study time and your sleep time. Uh ... most of the students at St. Olaf also have jobs outside of class. Sometimes the jobs are here on campus, on the college campus. And the money you earn is paid by the government and goes to pay for the tuition cost of St. Olaf. And other students have, other students have jobs off campus. It might be a waitress at a restaurant or uh ... work at a gas station or something like this, to earn some money to spend or to pay for a car, pay for a trip.

**Interviewer:** Uh ... so you just mentioned that they do part-time jobs in order to pay school fees or pay for books. Are there any other reasons that they do part-time jobs?

**Rachel:** Yeah. I think a lot of students, most students spend money on books or college tuition; they're paying for school. But also they need money to go out with their friends. They might have a car and they have to pay for the gas and insurance of the car um ... Because school is so expensive, also students have to take out loans and then they pay those off sooner.

## Text Two

**Interviewer:** The next question I'd like to ask is that, whether every student has a boyfriend or a girlfriend.

**Rachel:** That's a fun question. Um ... yeah, a lot of students have boyfriends or girlfriends. And you might start dating somebody and go out a few times, go to movies, go to dinner or something. And then, then uh ... you decide, you know, this isn't somebody that you're going to date much longer. And then you find somebody else. You go with them, you go dancing. Uh ... I think a lot of people are girlfriends or boyfriends, but not very serious.

**Interviewer:** OK, this means that they are not going to marry each other?

**Rachel:** No, probably not. I think most, most people have boyfriends or girlfriends and go out to have fun and not think about getting married.

**Interviewer:** So what do you think of your school life? You have studied, have spent four years studying at St. Olaf.

**Rachel:** Hum. Uh ... I'm really looking back now as a senior. I can see that I've had a lot of fun with my friends and I've learned a lot here at St. Olaf. Uh ... I think I'm more prepared to go out and start working. And I'm kind of excited about that. Freshman year, when I came, I didn't know anybody. And you leave your family for the first time, and you make all these new friends and have a lot of fun. And sophomore year you start to study a little bit harder. And you're still having fun with your friends. And then junior year, uh ... you can study overseas, or uh ... you're still spending time with your friends, but you're also working very hard on your studies.

**Interviewer:** So which country have you been to? You say junior year you began to go abroad.

**Rachel:** Hum. Uh ... I spent the first semester of this year teaching Art in Hongkong, China at an international school there.

**interviewer:** OK. Any other countries that you have been to?

**Rachel:** Yes. When I was uh ... in high school, my senior year, last year of high school, I went to Germany as an exchange student and lived in Berlin with a German family.

**Interviewer:** So what do you think your foreign experience helped you uh ... in study or in other aspects of life?

**Rachel:** Yeah ... I think it helped in lots of different areas. One of them is certainly my independence. And coming to college was not as difficult because I had already been away from my parents for some time in Germany. And I think speaking another language is really important, And uh ... making new friends, just learning about the different ways people live and do things.

**Interviewer:** So this is your senior year in college and you're going to graduate this semester. So uh ... have you found a job?

**Rachel:** Yes. I did find a job. After teaching Art in Hongkong, I realized that I like to teach overseas, and so I looked for a job in the international job market. I found one in Istanbul, Turkey. And so I'll be moving to Istanbul in September to teach Art at a primary school and teach fourth, fifth and sixth grades uh ... using English.

**III. Listen and choose the best answer to each question you hear.**

1. Which of the following is NOT mentioned by Rachel concerning what most students do when they date somebody?
2. In which year can university students have foreign experiences according to Rachel?
3. Where did Rachel go as an exchange student when she was in high school?

## Part Four Here's More

### Exercise

There are two types of universities in the USA, public and private. The public universities are state universities, the quality of which varies from state to state and from university to university within that state. Some of the state universities are specialized in certain fields of study, for example, the University of California at Davis is specialized in linguistics. Some are general universities with degrees offered in many fields. The University of California at Berkeley is such a university. Previously, anyone who graduated from a high school in a given state was automatically granted the right to study at that state's state university. However, in recent years the numbers of high school graduates who want to go on to university have risen so high that entrance exams are now required at most universities, both state and private. In addition, the so-called SAT exams are also usually required, and there is a minimum score that is necessary for university entrance. The SAT score required varies from university to university.

Most pupils graduate from high school and enter university at the age of 18. Education starts at age six, and there are a total of twelve years of primary and secondary school.

All universities charge tuition fees. If your parents pay taxes in a given state, and you yourself have lived in that state for at least a year previous to going to university, the tuition fees for a state university are quite low. Otherwise, they are fairly high, although not as high as the fees charged by private universities. Students have to buy books, but second-hand copies at low prices are usually readily available. All students under the age of 21 must live in dormitories on the university campus. These are usually large buildings with several bedrooms shared by two people, with a large communal shower room and WC facilities. A single, shared telephone is on every floor. Most students in the USA have mobile phones. Dormitory fees are cheaper than renting living space off campus, so that most students stay in dormitories even after they reach 21. Boys and girls live in the same building, but not on the same floor.

# Unit 11

# Anna in Australia

## Part Two Listen Now

### Text One

**Tutor:** Today I have with me Anna Cherney, who was a student at this college, er ... how long ago?

**Anna:** I was here one and a half, no, two years ago.

**Tutor:** Anna was a student in this English class when she was at the college. And she is here to tell us about the many problems facing a nonnative speaker in an Australian tertiary institution. What have you been doing since you graduated, Anna?

**Anna:** I ... was quite lucky when I left the college because I got a job pretty quickly with the local council. I'm still with them.

**Tutor:** Tell the class what course you took here at the college.

**Anna:** I originally wanted to work in advertising, but I found it was too hard because of my English. And so I changed my direction, and, well, I'm glad I did because I've now got an Associate Diploma in Nutritional Science, and that's how I managed to get a job with the council.

**Tutor:** What exactly do you do with the council?

**Anna:** I work with the chief dietitian, making sure that the "meals on wheels" provide good food for the older people in the community who can't get out of their flat or their house. It's a very demanding job but I like it.

**Tutor:** You deliver the food?

**Anna:** No, no. I spend most of my day in a laboratory at the council, but sometimes I talk to older people to find out if the food is tasty enough, and ... er ... if they like it. I spend a lot of time in the kitchens, too, making sure that the food is of good quality.

**Tutor:** What exactly were the problems when you first arrived at the college?

**Anna:** I was very shy, you know. I couldn't communicate with the students in my class because most of them were Australian ... my English was not very good. But I thought everything was OK, until I got the result of my first examination. The tutor was worried why I was so quiet in class. I told her it was because I was afraid to ask a question, and, anyway, she suggested that I talk to the school counselor.

**Tutor:** What advice did the counselor give?

**Anna:** Well, she was very kind and understanding, and I realized that I was doing the wrong course. You have to be extrovert, you know, outgoing. I think it's a personal thing with me. You had to give a lot of opinions, and I was shy. So, she suggested I ask more questions in class, so I made it a rule to ask at least one or two questions every lesson.

**Tutor:** So you swapped courses and began to talk more in class. Was there anything else that the counselor suggested?

**Anna:** Yes, she said I shouldn't live with students from my own country. I should share a house with some Australian students. So I did and my English improved much faster.

## Text Two

**Tutor:** Are there any problems that you currently have with English?

**Anna:** Oh, yes. I used to have problems with the technical vocabulary in my field, but you pick that up pretty quickly. Now, it's mostly ... I have difficulty trying to understand the colloquial language of Australians; the way they sometimes express themselves in everyday life is very strange.

**Tutor:** I see. How do you increase your vocabulary, for instance?

**Anna:** I listen to the radio a lot. Interviews on radio, talk-back programs, that sort of thing. I find that really helps me. It's better than just watching TV. And actually, I keep a journal of the expressions I hear. Some people collect stamps, and I collect new words and English expressions.

**Tutor:** Let's talk some more about your course at the college. Do you remember any study projects that you were involved in?

**Anna:** Er, let me see ... well, there was one study we made of the nutritional habits of Australian schoolchildren. We had to produce a questionnaire, for a group of 20 kids, and we discovered that, too many children either didn't have any breakfast at all, or else they ate foods for breakfast that were much too high in sugar. These are two major dietary problems.

**Tutor:** Why?

**Anna:** It's complicated, but breakfast is an important meal because your metabolic rate — the rate at which the body burns up food — is faster the earlier you begin eating in the day. So, if you want to have lots of energy, eat a good, balanced breakfast. Also, too much sugar in the diet can cause the blood sugar level to rise very quickly at first, and then drop too rapidly. For breakfast, this is bad because later you are more likely to feel sleepy and unable to concentrate. So, eat a good breakfast, you'll think better, concentrate better, and yes, you'll probably score better in your exams.

**Tutor:** Um, one last question. What about your future? Have you any immediate plans?

**Anna:** Well, in the short term I'll continue to work for the council and gain more experience there. I hope to get a position in a hospital, which would be much more challenging than my present job. After that, I ... er ... my long-term goal is ... I have a dream to open my own business — an agency providing nutritional advice and giving consultation — or ... I might have to go back to my own country instead and do what I can to improve the diet of my people at home. Modern influences are causing great changes to the traditional diet.

## Part Four Here's More

### Exercise One

1. **Ann:** And when would you like to move in?

   **Bill:** On the first of the next month.

   **Ann:** Okay. Are there any other amenities which you would like to have? For example, a dishwasher, a balcony, a swimming pool or central air conditioning?

   **Bill:** I would definitely like to have a dishwasher, and with summers like these, central air! A balcony is not that important. Oh, yes, two bathrooms would be nice.

2. **Receptionist:** Well, we ask applicants to apply no later than two months before the semester begins. This gives us time to process the application and issue the student's I-20.

   **Caller:** An I-20?

   **Receptionist:** Oh, an I-20 is a form that indicates that we are giving permission for the student to study in our program, and then the student takes this form to the US embassy in his or her home country to apply for the F-1 student visa.

3. **M:** What kind of differences have you noticed between teaching in the United States and in Chinese Hong Kong?

   **W:** There are many common points, but there are some important differences. The main difference is that, when I am teaching English in the US, I am teaching what's called "English as a second language" — "ESL." This means that the students are living in an environment where English is spoken.

4. **Librarian:** Can I help you?

   **Natalie:** Yes. I am a bit confused. My sociology class is supposed to read a chapter in a book called Sociology and the Modern Age. According to the syllabus, the book is in the library, but I haven't been able to find it.

   **Librarian:** Do you have your syllabus with you? May I see it?

   **Natalie:** Yes, uh ... I put it in the front of my sociology notebook. Oh, here it is.

   **Librarian:** Let me see. Oh yes, your professor has placed this book on reserve. That means you cannot find it on the shelves in its usual place. You need to go to a special room called the reserve room. It's down the hall and to the right.

### Exercise Two

1. Currently, doctors use a method called endoscopy to provide images of the small intestines. An endoscope is a long thin tube with a small camera on the end. Doctors use endoscopy to identify growths, cancer and causes of bleeding. Doctors place the endoscope down a patient's throat to look at the small intestine.
2. The most important distinction to make is between the psychological (or mental) shock which may follow a physically or emotionally traumatic experience, and physiological (or circulatory) shock,

which is a dramatic reduction in blood flow through the body which if untreated may progress to collapse, coma and even death.

3. However, a number of people will find it harder to get back to normal and may develop PTSD, Post-Traumatic Stress Disorder.
4. Have you always wanted to invest, but didn't know where to get started? We're here today to present you with some basic guidelines to smart investing, for your future. Number one is to have clear goals. Decide how many years you will invest for, and what your needs will be in the future. Number two is to understand the range of possibilities. You'll want a diversified portfolio: one with a mix of stocks, mutual funds, bonds, and cash. It's a jungle out there. Each of these products has different risks associated with them and also different potential rewards. Understand them before you buy, so there won't be any big surprises later.

# Unit 12

# Working on Board the Plane

## Part Two Listen Now

### Text One

**Sue:** Good afternoon and welcome to "Working Lives." My name is Sue Holt. This week we continue our series by looking at a job that is often thought of as adventurous, exotic, and highly desirable. We're going to take a behind-the-scenes look at the airline hospitality industry. What is the reality behind the smart uniform and ever ready smile of the flight attendant? We're lucky enough to have in the studio Julie Nevard, who works for Australian Airways, and is a senior member of the cabin crew staff. Thank you for finding the time to speak to us. I know that you must have a busy schedule.

**Julie:** My pleasure. Yes, it is a very full-time job but I think you realize that very early in your career.

**Sue:** How long have you been involved in in-flight hospitality?

**Julie:** Well, I trained for a year at the Australian Airways Training School, and ... I'd already taken an Associate Diploma in Hospitality and Tourism at TAFE after I left school ... so all in all ... about 5 years ... no, more like 6 years.

**Sue:** So your training was at TAFE?

**Julie:** Well, yes, the preliminary training, but then the Australian Airways Training Course in Darwin was a more specialized hospitality course. I suppose you could call the TAFE Associate Diploma my major professional qualification.

**Sue:** I see. Now tell me, is the job as glamorous as most people believe?

**Julie:** Absolutely not! Oh, of course, there are many good things about the job. You know, you never know where you might be going. For example, I still get excited when I see the new roster for the first time, knowing I'll soon be off somewhere I haven't been before, on a new route. The best thing, of course, is that all the time I'm meeting new people. But people don't realize that what I get to see most of is the inside of hotel rooms, and most hotel rooms are pretty similar.

Also, it's like, I'm working, but the majority of my passengers are on holiday. Sometimes it's hard to deal with all their demands.

**Sue:** Then tell me, what is your main responsibility during a flight?

**Julie:** That's hard to say really. Well, we're responsible for all the needs and demands of each and every passenger, for up to 10 hours on some long haul flights. Not to mention the safety of the plane and all the passengers. I suppose, if I have to come up with a single answer, it'd be passenger comfort.

### III. Listen and choose the best answer to each question you hear.

1. How long has Julie been involved in in-flight hospitality?
2. How did Julie become qualified as a flight attendant?
3. Which of the following is NOT the reason that Julie gets excited when she sees the new roster for the first time?

## Text Two

**Sue:** Do you find yourself going to the same places often?

**Julie:** There are four or five major destinations that we fly to more regularly than others. Yes, I've got to know some cities very well.

**Sue:** Oh, really? Which destinations are those?

**Julie:** Well, there's London, Hong Kong, Bali, LAX ...

**Sue:** That's in New York?

**Julie:** Los Angles ... these are the most frequent destinations with Australian Airways.

**Sue:** So with all that travel, how do you deal with the constant changing of time zones?

**Julie:** It's something you just have to get used to. Oh, everybody in the industry has a special tip to beat jet lag. But me? I just make sure that I am regularly changing the time on my watch. I find that if I change the time little by little and fairly frequently, well, that seems to work well for me. You see, I have two watches: the one I'm constantly adjusting and the one with the original time at departure.

**Sue:** That sounds like a good idea. So, have you seen many changes in the type of services you offer?

**Julie:** Oh, yes. These days the competition is much tougher. I suppose the result is that the consumer, the traveler, has a much better deal. Well the seats are bigger, more comfortable than they were 10 years ago; the in-flight entertainment; the films ... now they are all recent release blockbusters. They weren't 10 years ago. But the two biggest improvements have been to do with the smoking restrictions and the upgrading of the meals.

**Sue:** Oh right, tell me about these two changes.

**Julie:** Yes, the restriction on smoking on some routes and the banning of smoking on others has had a two-fold benefit. Firstly, the atmosphere is much more pleasant, and, secondly, the fire risk is greatly reduced. You know, we used to have people dropping cigarettes, burning the seats. A dreadful fire risk. Can you imagine?

**Sue:** Terrible.

**Julie:** I, for one, never understood why anyone was ever allowed to smoke on aeroplanes in the first place.

**Sue:** Um ... and the meals?

**Julie:** Ah, with so many carriers vying for passengers on the same route, you just have to offer more. Vegetarian meals, choice of two hot meals, interesting, exotic, gourmet food — all this is now commonplace in our economy class galleys. And for the business and first-class passengers, the food is as good as in any world-class restaurant — top chefs, great presentation, nutritious ingredients ... really quite lovely.

**Sue:** And finally, what advice or words of warning would you give to school leavers considering a career in this industry?

**Julie:** That's a difficult question. Let me think ... I'd say think long and hard about why you want to do it. It's not all glamorous, and it can be very hard work. It affects your family and your social life. I mean, I don't have any social life to speak of, unless it's with my colleagues at the airline. But, all the same, it remains a rewarding and challenging career. You certainly never get bored.

**Sue:** Julie, it's been fascinating talking to you. Thank you for your time.

**III. Listen and choose the best answer to each question you hear.**

1. Which of the following places is NOT a major destination that Julie frequently flies to?
2. How many changes have taken place in the type of in-flight services according to Julie?
3. What is the reason leading to improvement in the type of services offered by the airline?

## Part Four Here's More

### Exercise One

1. W: Good evening, Professor David. My name is Susan Gray. I'm with the local newspaper. Do you mind if I ask you a few questions?
   M: Not at all. Go ahead, please.
   Q: What is Susan Gray?
2. W: I heard you got full marks in the math exam. Congratulations!
   M: Thanks. I'm sure you also did a good job.
   Q: What's the probable relationship between the two speakers?
3. W: This is Mrs. Jones. My heater is not getting any power and the temperature is going to get down below freezing. Could you come over and fix it?
   M: This is our busiest time of the year, but I'll speak to one of our men about getting over there sometime today.
   Q: Who has Mrs. Jones called to come over?
4. M: Can you bill me later?
   W: I'm sorry, I can't. You're a new patient, so the fee for the first examination is due now. You can pay by cash, credit card or check.
   Q: Who is the woman?
5. M: My family and I will be leaving. Is there anything we need to do to the apartment before we leave?
   W: If you want your fifty-dollar deposit back, you'll have to clean the stove and the refrigerator. Also, we ask that you vacuum carefully before leaving.

Q: What does the woman do for a living?

6. W: Should we give her anything special to drink?
   M: Yes, lots of liquids, especially clear juices.
   Q: What is the probable relationship between the two speakers?
7. M: I have a terrible cold, and I can't stop coughing. What do you take for a cold, Linda?
   W: Well, I usually rely on old home remedies like honey and whiskey.
   Q: Who is the woman?
8. W: The drain is clogged again and there's water all over the bathroom floor.
   M: We'll have to call Mr. Morris right away.
   Q: What job does Mr. Morris probably have?
9. W: Hi, Mr. Talcott. Is my prescription ready?
   M: It's right here. Just follow these directions and take one pill right after each meal.
   Q: What's the man's occupation?
10. M: The food was great, and I've never had better service.
    W: Thank you, sir. I'll pass your compliments on to the chef and thanks again for the tip.
    Q: What's the woman's job?

## Exercise Two

1. It's very hard work. The patient is usually nervous, so you have to be bright and cheerful, however you're feeling. And you spend most of the day on your feet. But it's quite creative — making people's teeth look good. And when you do a good job, it's very satisfying. It takes a certain skill — you need to be good with your hands. You can't afford to make mistakes!
2. You have to have good, fast, accurate shorthand and typing. You've got to be good at English and spelling — and there are so many other things. You need to be reliable, and loyal to your boss. And you need a sense of humour — particularly in my case, because I work for a TV producer.
3. It takes a lot of energy and hard work, and I'm usually exhausted at the end of the day. But I enjoy it. You don't have to have any special talents. I don't have any. But I suppose I do know how to do quite a few things — I'm a cook, and a cleaner, and a nurse when the kids are ill, and I decorate the place, so you could say I'm a painter ... and I don't get paid for any of it. But I never really thought about a career ... maybe when the children are grown up ...
4. You have to be good at working in a team, and you've got to be able to make quick decisions. And of course, you need to know how to use the equipment properly. It's funny. When I was a kid, I was scared of heights. And in my job, you've got to go up a ten-storey building on a ladder. I suppose it takes courage. But when you're saving lives, you don't think about being afraid. I care about people — that's why I do it.
5. Well, you have to have a friendly personality, and you've got to look good. And I have to be able to speak Spanish. But it's not as glamorous as you think. You have to look after the passengers and serve drinks and be a waitress and an interpreter, and all the time you have to keep smiling. And that's not easy when you've been in the air for hours, with no time to eat or rest.

# Unit 13

# Achieving Career Success

## Part Two Listen Now

### Text One

For the last 17 years Ross has been a very successful small businessman. For some business is a game they play to win; for others they value the freedom and choices that success brings. Ross is of the latter type; he found being an employee or an employer took too much of his effort pleasing co-workers rather than clients. Ross runs his own business as salesman, manager and employee. He has done extremely well for himself, and for his customers.

We are proud to present this recent interview of Ross Rayburn by the Rector of Bastiat Free University.

**BFU:** Ross, do you have a "most important advice" for a person considering working for themselves?

**RR:** No. What is most important will vary with each person. Some will need to discover themselves first, others just need to get off their butts and start. If someone is not confident of their abilities, I would encourage them to get a sales job in a retail establishment. Promotions come quickly in retail, they will get experience in all sorts of business disciplines, sales, buying, inventory control, income statements, and lots of other important knowledge. They will also get the chance to enter management and discover if they enjoy that relationship. If they decide to go out on their own, they will have the basics for success along with a knowledge of their own strengths and weaknesses.

**BFU:** So what makes the difference in starting styles, and how would a person find where they fit?

**RR:** Personalities. Some learn best getting face to face with clients, others need to get face to face with themselves first. Everyone needs to keep learning and challenging themselves if they expect to be successful. There are many good inspirational books or biographies of successful people that a person can read. I am usually reading three or four books at a time; I do make sure the book I read before bed is inspirational.

I also listen to motivational tapes or books on tape in the car. Music is nice, but it will not help me develop a winning outlook. A lot of your ability to apply yourself comes from your own determination; you develop that by immersing yourself in positive information.

**BFU:** I hear you are saying about reading biographies. When I read about George Muller I found out a great deal about the flexibility of faith, and its application. Is there one biography you have read that stands out?

**RR:** Ford. Henry Ford. An original thinker and a great success at accomplishing what he set out to do. He had a top notch group of engineers, many of the best. He told them he wanted a V8 engine, they said it couldn't be done. He kept going back and asking how they were doing on that V8, they kept saying it was impossible. After a year or so he asked, and someone had an idea of how it might be done. It was done.

**BFU:** Was there anything else that impressed you about Ford?

**RR:** There was a point where Ford was going through competency hearings. Someone wanted to put him away and take over. They kept asking Ford basic questions, as he only had a third grade education, he had no idea what the answers were. Ford finally got fed up with their trying to show a lack of education that meant he was not competent to manage his affairs. Ford said, "I manage a huge company, I can push a button on my desk, and get the top expert in the world to answer any question I want answered. I don't need to know the answers, I know how to get an answer if I need it." Ford knew his job was to think, and ask new questions; those with the education to have the appropriate answers could be employed to answer them.

## III. Listen and choose the best answer to each question you hear.

1. Why does Ross work for himself?
2. Which of the following is NOT mentioned by Ross as an advantage for people to work in a retail establishment?
3. What should a person do if he expects to be successful according to Ross?

## Text Two

**BFU:** How well were you prepared when you went out on your own?

**RR:** I started my business at the same time as 9 other sales people, of the 10 of us I was the least qualified. Within a short time I was the only one left. There is a huge amount of work required when starting a business. I am extremely lucky that my wife and I are on the same page. She knows how important it is for me to stay glued to my desk, or sometimes the kitchen table, without interruptions. It took 4 months before I was making enough to cover all my bills, and a bit beyond for goodies. Those were 4 months of 6 or 7 days a week, working from early morning to late night. I kept that schedule for quite a while as I built my business, and I still wake early to get a few uninterrupted hours of working before the world starts humming.

**BFU:** Once you have started sales, how can you be most effective?

**RR:** The key is getting face to face with your clients. Drop by, even if all you do is hand them a business card. I've never had a client act upset that I've shown up, although sometimes if they are busy all I do is say Hi. Frequently they will say, "Hold on a minute Ross, there is something I want to talk to you about." That doesn't happen when you call for an appointment.

**BFU:** Ross, talk a bit about the pleasure of working for yourself.

**RR:** I'm happy to. When I worked for a boss and a regular paycheck my wife had to push me out of bed in the mornings. I hated the alarm clock, I hated the sunrise. After I quit and started working for myself everything changed. It didn't take long; the first morning I jumped out of bed, set myself up, and started going. Now the great part: I was doing exactly the same job; the difference was I was doing it for myself. Instead of a dribble of a paycheck, everything I made belonged to me.

**BFU:** How do you organize yourself?

**RR:** I'm a firm believer in the 80/20 rule. 80% of your sales come from 20% of your clients. The key is to put 80% of your effort into that 20% that are your best customers. Many companies ignore their clients while they beat the bushes for new customers.

**BFU:** You have established that it will take hard work to develop a business. Anyone can see that you have enjoyed the rewards of your efforts. Other than the lazy, or those without the freedom to dedicate themselves to the task, what else would limit someone from opening their own business?

**RR:** You hit that right. There are a few personality traits that might disqualify someone from seeking the freedom of their own company. I believe however that everyone can sell. Selling is easy and natural; you talk and find out what is best for the client, then you help them make a decision that is to their benefit.

**BFU:** Any final thoughts, Ross?

**RR:** Yes. If you want to be successful and stay successful, remember one thing: All business is long term.

**BFU:** Thank you Mr. Rayburn.

## Part Four Here's More

### Exercise One

1. Michael's house is a stone's throw from the library.
2. Kate was really feeling down in the dumps about her latest chemistry assignment.
3. In writing ability, Margaret's head and shoulders above the rest of the class.
4. Mary's suggestion to the teacher was out of the question.
5. He has a job on the side, preparing the laboratory every day for the next experiments.
6. As long as Lita's visiting California, she'll make a point of seeing San Francisco.
7. At first, many people didn't like that kind of music, but after a while it caught on.
8. Bill was on the verge of speeding when he saw the patrolman.
9. Although groceries were high, the family managed to get by on sixty dollars a week.
10. After talking to your advisor, you may sign up for classes.

### Exercise Two

1. M: We've been at it long enough for Sunday evening. Besides, the printer is running out of paper.
   W: OK, Let's call it a night and go out for a snack before everything closes.
   Q: What does the woman mean?
2. M: Let's start our preparations for the party by putting up a couple of posters in the student center.
   W: I'd say that anything that gets the ball rolling would be helpful at this point.
   Q: What does the woman mean?
3. W: I hear you're taking an advanced physics course this semester. How's it going?
   M: I think I've bitten off more than I can chew.
   Q: What does the man mean?
4. M: Look, I'm sorry I didn't turn up for the match yesterday, but it wasn't really my fault, you know.
   W: It's all very well saying it wasn't your fault, but thanks to you we lost 10 to 1.
   Q: What do we learn from the conversation?
5. M: Look, the view is fantastic. Could you take a picture of me with the lake in the background?
   W: I am afraid I just ran out of film.
   Q: What do we learn from the conversation?
6. M: Don't you talk down to me, Wendy. Whether you like it or not, I know just as much about the subject as you do, if not more.
   W: But Jim, I really think my experience has been much more relevant.
   Q: What does Jim object to?
7. M: Jessica, could you forward this e-mail to all the club members?

W: Sorry, the computer broke down this morning. I'll do it for you as soon as I have it fixed.
Q: What does the woman imply?

8. M: Let's cut a slice of this loaf. I'm starving.
W: Hold your horses. It still needs to cool. I promise you it will taste better afterwards.
Q: What does the woman mean?

9. M: Karen volunteered to present the report for our group this afternoon.
W: I certainly wouldn't want to be in her shoes.
Q: What does the woman mean?

10. M: Well, this is a pleasant surprise. It seems to me we ran into each other here last week too.
W: You and I must have the same idea. The only way to beat the crowds when you do the grocery shopping on Saturday is to be here when they open up at 9:00 sharp.
Q: Why did both of them do grocery shopping at 9:00 sharp?

# Unit 14 Farming

## Part Two Listen Now

### Text One

**Interviewer:** Cattle raising and … and beef in the US is … is big business, isn't it?

**Bob Becker:** Yes, it's the largest business — cattle business.

**Interviewer:** It must be a very profitable business then …

**Bob Becker:** Uh … not necessarily.

**Interviewer:** It's not necessarily a … a profitable business?

**Bob Becker:** At times, it's not profitable. Your production costs get — it's a supply and demand market, and if your supply is larger than your demand, why at times —

**Interviewer:** So the price is fluctuating all the time …

**Bob Becker:** Right. It fluctuates, and it can get below production costs.

**Interviewer:** But you never know … For instance, next year, you … you don't know what it'll bring on the market.

**Bob Becker:** No, it takes, technically, … it takes a year and a half from the time you breed the cow, until you get the calf, until the calf's marketable.

**Interviewer:** Uh-huh …

**Bob Becker:** You've got a year, to a year and a half, tied up there …

**Interviewer:** So, you're making an investment all the time …

**Bob Becker:** Right. So you're not sure.

**Interviewer:** It sounds like it might be a very … uh … insecure kind of existence. Wonder why it is that people want to be farmers or ranchers then …

**Bob Becker:** I think the majority of it is you like it. It's one thing … it's a breed of people. They like it. If you don't like what you're doing, why …

**Interviewer:** What is there about it? You live essentially in a rural area. Doesn't that feeling of isolation ever bother you?

**Bob Becker:** No. It's getting too crowded …

**Interviewer:** Too crowded!

**Bob Becker:** Too many people!

**Interviewer:** I can see that, for instance, in a city, you have … uh … restaurants to go to, movies, theaters — all kinds of things available to people … a lot of conveniences which you don't have in the more rural areas. What do people who farm, ranch, do for recreation and relaxation, for instance, uh …

**Bob Becker:** Well, I think a lot of it is if you're a livestock raiser, you … you just … you'll go check your cows in the evening instead of going to a movie.

**Interviewer:** Uh-huh.

**Bob Becker:** That's as much recreation as going — driving through a …

**Interviewer:** Uh-hm …

**Bob Becker:** … bunch of cows, and if you like them, why, you … you enjoy that.

**Interviewer:** In terms of the way of life … uh … to a lot of people, it would … it would seem that it's a very hard life. It means a lot of hard work. I mean, you have … you have a schedule — whether you feel like it or not, you have to … uh … get out and feed animals, and so forth. Would you regard that as one of the difficult things about it, or is that …

**Bob Becker:** No …

**Interviewer:** … just sort of … part of it …?

**Bob Becker:** For me, if I had to go to a desk every morning, that'd kill me …

### III. Listen and choose the best answer to each question you hear.

1. What business is the largest in the rural area of the US?
2. How long does it take from breeding a cow to getting a marketable calf?
3. According to this interview, how do farmers feel about their life?
4. According to this interview, what does a farmer usually do for recreation?
5. What do many people think of a farmer's life?

## Text Two

**Bob Becker:** I think … uh … for a wife, the same as a husband, they like it, or they wouldn't marry a farmer or a rancher.

**Interviewer:** Uh-huh.

**Bob Becker:** They'd … or else, they'd get out. That's … I think it's — it's not all wives. Some of them are just like suburban housewives.

**Interviewer:** Uh-hm …

**Bob Becker:** They cook the meals, and they clean the house and that's it — take care of the kids …

**Interviewer:** Have you known … have you known some situations like that?

**Bob Becker:** Oh, yeah, I know situations like that!

**Interviewer:** Sharon, what … uh — Is there a problem of … uh … on the feeling of security?

**Sharon Becker:** What kind of security are you talking about — financial security?

**Interviewer:** Uh ... yeah, financial security ... Uh ... the thing is up and down. You don't know what the market's going to bring ... uh ... for beef. You work all year, and so forth ... uh ... Is there any problem of that sort?

**Sharon Becker:** Sure, there's the problem of security. Especially, if you've had one or two bad years. You feel awfully insecure ...

**Interviewer:** Uh-huh.

**Sharon Becker:** If you've borrowed money to ... to buy a farm or ... uh ... to operate — borrowed money to operate, and ... and there's no money coming in, you feel awfully insecure.

**Interviewer:** Uh-huh ...

**Sharon Becker:** But you can always sell your equity in your ranch. So it isn't complete disaster.

**Interviewer:** So ... it's not something that bothers you terribly. I mean, that ... you ... it's a fact of life. It's sort of ...

**Sharon Becker:** Something you live with, yeah ...

**Interviewer:** Part of ... uh ... part of the thing. The role of the wife in this situation is quite different than ... uh ... that of a suburban housewife. You don't have much free time, do you?

**Sharon Becker:** No.

**Interviewer:** Because, essentially, you work in much the same way that your ... that your husband does ...

**Sharon Becker:** Yes. I'm usually with him.

**Interviewer:** How do you handle uh ... the whole family-life situation — children? You're out almost as much as ... uh ... as a working mother in the city, aren't you?

**Sharon Becker:** Yes. The only difference is we're together.

**Interviewer:** That is, ... the children too ...

**Sharon Becker:** The children too. When they're not in school ... when they were small, they were with us — when they were very small, of course, I didn't go out as much.

**Interviewer:** Do you feel that there are advantages in growing up in this way?

**Sharon Becker:** Yeah, I definitely feel that there's ... there's advantages. There are disadvantages too, but I think the ... uh ... the advantages far outweigh the disadvantages.

**Interviewer:** What are some of those ... uh ... advantages you think the children have?

**Sharon Becker:** The advantages ...?

**Interviewer:** Uh-huh.

**Sharon Becker:** Well ... uh ... they're a lot more self-reliant. They learn to work. Uh ... they learn responsibility ...

**Interviewer:** Uh-huh ...

**Sharon Becker:** They learn a lot about life by being continually in life ... uh ... with animals, and ... uh ... I think it makes them ... uh ... They grow up!

## Part Four Here's More

### Exercise

1. **Interviewer:** John, as a baseball player, is there any problem with a sort of feeling insecure?

John: Yeah, there is. Especially, like I said — my first year. I disciplined myself and worked hard. And I realize that I have to work hard to stay here. And there is insecurity.

Interviewer: You're under contract ...

John: Right, I'm under contract. But that doesn't necessarily — I mean, they could send me down tomorrow. They could do whatever they wanted with me.

2. **Interviewer:** Is there any move among ranchers or farmers to ... to organize at all? I mean ... uh ... labor unions.

**Bob:** Not ... not labor-union-wise ... uh ... Most ranchers and farmers don't want anything to do with it.

**Interviewer:** With unions?

**Bob:** Because we hire ... that labor we hire, why, and the price of our products, doesn't warrant union-paid-scale labor.

3. **Interviewer:** A lot of people think of you and remember you because of the Daniel Boone series...

**Mckennon:** Right. That was a series uh ...

**Interviewer:** ... which, I suppose, has probably been on television all around the world.

**Mckennon:** It has been in many, many countries ...

4. **Senn:** Everybody always has this misconception that female policemen don't do the same thing as men do, you know. I've worked ...

**Interviewer:** That's not true?

**Senn:** That is not true! I've worked my share of graveyard shifts, and, you know, split shifts, and double-backs and no days off ...

5. **Interviewer:** I wonder if there's a difference in work attitude, in general — working for yourself or working for a big company.

**Hamlin:** Yes ...uh... Sure there's a difference. I guess that part of it is that ... that you're more ... uh.. conscious of time when you work for a big company ...

6. **Interviewer:** There's something sort of ... uh ... impersonal about a big company to a lot of people.

**Hamlin:** Well, it is impersonal in that ... uh ... probably just a small percentage of the employees know the top management. Uh ... the people that work for me ... uh ... I don't think any of them have ever met the controller of the company — who is ... is their boss!

**Interviewer:** Hmm ...

**Hamlin:** And none of them probably ever seen the president of the company!

7. **Interviewer:** Sara, as a veterinarian, what sort of problems have you ... uh ... had to deal with?

**Sara:** What sort of problems! I've seen a lot of ...

**Interviewer:** Aren't you —?

**Sara:** ... things that I'm supposed to see once in a lifetime! And I've seen them in two months.

8. **Sara:** I've heard it said ... uh ... there was one lady that bought a coffin for her dog, and for six months she ...

**Interviewer:** A coffin?

**Sara:** A coffin for her dog — it was a thousand-dollar coffin. And then for six months, she slept on the floor with the dog.

# Unit 15

# People Skills

## Part Two Listen Now

### Text One

**Irene:** So we're gonna talk with Debra Benton. She majored in economics and in finance, and she landed out of college a sales job with an expense account, a salary, travel, everything you can imagine, and then she got fired. Now this book and everything in her life that came after, that came from that one firing. So thanks so much for joining us, Debra, and thanks for writing the book, *Lions Don't Need to Roar*. Is there a formula for success? I mean, is there a ... is it 'cause it's something that can be learned, or are you born with it?

**Debra:** You are born with it and you can relearn it. The problem is we unlearn it when we get educated and socialized. And we go to school, and we want to, y'know, move up. We get out of school, we get a job, we wanna be professional, and we end up looking boring and constipated, trying to be taken seriously. And a lot that we had when we were young is what we need to succeed now but we've lost.

**Irene:** So how do we get it back? I mean, how are these skills learned? You are a consultant: you have your own company. As I say, it all came from this firing. You got fired and you...I'm sure you were stunned, y'know. "Why would someone fire me? I'm young. I'm attractive. I'm smart. I'm ..."

**Debra:** ... hardworking, honest.

**Irene:** All that stuff, and suddenly you're out on the streets, and so you figure out why. You said you lacked the people skills.

**Debra:** My boss said I lacked people skills, which was a surprise, but nonetheless others, many listeners have had experiences in their work where they were told, "there's just poor chemistry between you," or "he leaves a bad taste in your mouth," or "just, he's not dynamic enough," or "she just doesn't fit in." And what it really is: someone is probably very competent, but they haven't learned how to show and project their competence. And being good and not projecting it is no better than being good in my experience. And you can relearn these things but still be very genuine.

**Irene:** What are some tricks to ... to looking confident, even when you're not?

**Debra:** Skills vs. tricks!

**Irene:** Oh, sorry, sorry. Bad words, but ...

**Debra:** That's okay. But they can sound like tricks, because when we analyze them, they can. But really it is a skill when it becomes a habit. Walking into a room, you can walk in hurriedly, race towards the person you're gonna shake hands, sit down, put your hands in your lap, ready for the first question to be fired at you, okay, or you can walk in, pause ever so slightly, non-verbally announce, "I'm here." Give him or her a split second to put down what they're doing, look up, maybe stand up, give you the due attention. As you approach them, if you take a little longer, you don't dawdle of course, but just don't hurry like you're anxious, and approach him, pause, perhaps shake hands, hold on a split second longer. Don't just do a flea-flicker handshake like a politician, y'know, ready to go to the next person.

**III. Listen and choose the best answer to each question you hear.**

1. What did Debra major in when she studied in the college?
2. Why do we need to relearn the skills for success?
3. Which of the statements does NOT show a lack of people skills?
4. Which statement is true according to Debra?

## Text Two

**Irene:** How important is a handshake?

**Debra:** In our culture, we "do business on a handshake basis," right? I mean, million-dollar deals are figuratively done in a handshake. Actually it's the first time you get to touch. It enables them to hear your name, you hear their name; it sets the whole tone.

**Irene:** What about names? I won't use the word "tricks" again. What are … what are some skills about remembering names? Someone once told me that what you are doing when introduced is so busily listening to make sure your name is being pronounced correctly that you often miss the other person's name. And certainly I've been in gatherings where five seconds later I truly can't remember the name of the person I was just introduced to and I feel so bad.

**Debra:** Right. You and I and the listeners, we're intelligent people: we would remember the name — that's easy — if we heard it. But think about it: you're shaking hands, you're a little self-conscious, self-aware of how you're coming across. You are saying your name, like you just said, and you didn't even hear their name. It's not that you didn't remember it: you didn't hear it. So obviously listen for it, if you slow down, like I've suggested, and take a little more time, you'll likely hear it. Shortly thereafter, you could use it in the conversation. And if you fear forgetting it, you can write it down when you walk away from that conversation. But listening for it — hearing is the first step.

**Irene:** Is it shameful to say "I'm sorry, I didn't get your name" ?

**Debra:** Absolutely not. And another way is when you meet them again, you can just extend your hand and say, "Hello, Debra Benton …"

**Irene:** Give them your name …

**Debra:** Right, and that will invite … And again, honest with a pleasant attitude is fine. Say, " You know, we met, and there were so many interesting people I met the other night. I can't remember everyone's name, I'm sorry, uh …" and kind of stop like that, and they'll say, "Well, Joe Blow."

**Irene:** Mm-hmm. Sure. What about people who just walk up and say, "Hi, you remember me, don't you?" You've had that happen to you.

**Debra:** Right. And I might say, "I do, and your face is so familiar, and my — I've just blocked your name" …

**Irene:** And then that … that really …

**Debra:** … which is true, which is honest, versus skipping around and acting like, "oh yes, oh yes" and like you know it, and …

**Irene:** And then of course your mind is going a mile a minute, you're not paying any attention to any clues that might be offered in the conversation, 'cause your mind is racing back through all the gatherings, all the office parties, all — whatever you've done in the last year, I mean you're sort of going nuts.

## Part Four Here's More

### Exercise One

1. She sat two rows in front of us. She had a bright yellow shirt on.
2. Would you mind my sitting here?
3. And I want to see if his band can play at my birthday party.
4. I've had enough. I don't know what to think of her anymore.
5. Mary looks so different now.
6. I heard that you just quit. I just can't believe it.
7. The waiter repeated, "Cash or charge?" But the foreign visitor still couldn't understand him.
8. I'm throwing out the food that made you sick at dinner the other night.
9. I got you the book you wanted. Here it is.
10. This test ranks your abilities.
11. She made those rolls you like. So why not come and have some?
12. He's trying to get hold of you.

### Exercise Two

**A short conversation**

A: Your lunch order is /lun-tʃɔː-dəz/ here. Turkey sandwich for Mrs. Jones.
B: She's in a /ʃɪ-zɪ-nə/ meeting.
A: Tuna club for Betty.
B: She's on /ʃɪ-zɒn/ the phone.
A: What about /wɒ-də-bau/ hot ham and cheese /hæ-mə-tʃiːz/?
B: That's mine. How much is it?
A: That'll be four and a /fɔː-rə-nə/ half bucks.
B: Here's five. Keep the change.
A: Thanks. If it's OK /fɪ-tsə-keɪ/, I'll just wait for the other ladies.
B: Sure, have a seat.

**A song: Country Roads**

Almost heaven
West Virginia
Blue Ridge Mountains
Shenandoah River
Life is old there
Older than the trees
Younger than the mountains
Growing like a breeze

Country roads take me home
To the place I belong
West Virginia
Mountain Mama

Take me home country roads

All my memories
Gather round her
Miner's lady
Stranger to blue water
Dark and dusty
Painted on the sky
Misty taste of moonshine
Teardrop in my eyes

Country roads take me home
To the place I belong
West Virginia
Mountain Mama
Take me home country roads

I hear her voice in the morning hours
She calls me
The radio reminds me of my home far away
And driving down the road
I get a feeling
That I should have been home
Yesterday, yesterday

Country roads take me home
To the place I belong
West Virginia
Mountain Mama
Take me home country roads

# Unit 16 Magic Disney World

## Part Two Listen Now

### Text One

**Presenter:** Walt Disney is well known as the creator of Mickey Mouse and the inventor of Disneyland and Walt Disney World, but his creations are better known than his life. Peter Spencer is the author of a new book about Disney. What was Walt Disney's background?

**Peter:** Walter Elias Disney was born in 1901 in Chicago but actually he was brought up in a small town in the Midwest near Kansas City, Missouri, which incidentally was later used as the model for Main Street USA in Disneyland. Um … he first studies cartooning, you know, by doing a correspondence course. During the First World War he worked as a … a driver for the American Red Cross but after the war he returned to Kansas City where he met a guy called Ub Iwerks. Now they … er … started to work together on a series of experimental-type films … um … and after a while they set off to California to join Walt's elder brother Roy who was living there in Los Angeles.

**Presenter:** When did Mickey Mouse first appear?

**Peter:** Ah, well, Disney and Iwerks first invented a character called Oswald the Rabbit but then in 1928 a new character was born: cheerful, sometimes rather naughty, energetic mouse with large funny ears. Yes, it was Mickey and he appeared for the first time in the first talking cartoon film, called *Steamboat Willie*. Er … not many people know this but Walt Disney actually provided the voice for Mickey. By the way, he was almost called "Mortimer Mouse," which doesn't have the same kind of ring to it, or does it?

Well, Roy and Walt gathered a team of artists … er … illustrators together … um … by this time Ub Iwerks had left them and started his own company. This was in 1930, and Disney Studios, as they called themselves, starting … started to produce the famous short cartoons with … starring Mickey and Minnie and Donald Duck and Pluto and Goofy. Er … Roy was the business manager and driving force behind the company … er … making it very profitable and Walt was more the … er … imaginative, creative part of the partnership.

## Text Two

**Presenter:** What kind of man was Walt Disney?

**Peter:** Well, according to the artists who worked for him, Walt actually couldn't draw very well … er … most of the characters were actually drawn by Iwerks, but apparently he was an amazing storyteller. He would act out the stories of films, doing all the voices and actions to show the illustrators what he wanted them to do, and then they had to go off and try to recreate his visualizations.

**Presenter:** The most famous cartoon of all was *Snow White* — and the best I still think.

**Peter:** Mm, yeah, it was the first feature-length cartoon and it was released in … er … 1938. Now, *Snow White and the Seven Dwarfs* required two million drawings and took three years' work to make. Um … obviously it was … er … very expensive, particularly for those times. By the way, the British film censor gave it an Adult certificate because he thought that it would be too frightening for little children to see on their own.

**Presenter:** That was followed by …?

**Peter:** Er … that was followed by *Pinocchio* and *Fantasia* in 1940, *Dumbo* in 1941. And … er … the Disney Studios also started making … um … some rather low-budget live action feature films for children … er … something which the other studios didn't dare risk doing. Er … some of his films mixed live action with cartoons — er … I'm thinking about *Mary Poppins*, which I think we've probably all seen, made in 1964, where cartoon characters and … and the real life actors appeared together on screen and talked and danced and sang together.

Disney was one of the first to see the potential of television, all the other studios were afraid of this medium. Um ... so he started to produce films directly for television and ... and now of course there's a Disney Channel showing only Disney films.

**Presenter:** And then he dreamt up Disneyland, didn't he?

**Peter:** Ah, "dreamt" is the right word. Disneyland was a creation of the land of his dreams: safe, happy, clean, fairy tale world with its own Magic Kingdom. The original Disneyland was opened in Los Angles in 1955 and it cost $17 million.

Walt died in 1966 but he was already working on plans for the Disney World in Orlando, Florida, which opened in 1971, and the EPCOT Center near Walt Disney World — that's the "Experimental Prototype Community of Tomorrow, " by the way. And there's also a ... a Tokyo Disneyland, which was opened in ... um ... 1983.

**Presenter:** And ... and now there's even an Euro Disneyland near Paris, I think.

**Peter:** Yes, that's right. Um ... and the Disney Studios still continue to produce films in the ... the house style, the Walt Disney style and presumably it always will. Disney's films appealed ... um ... and still do appeal to children of all ages, but people often criticize them for their lack of taste and they say they're vulgar. But Disney said, "I've never called this art. It's show business and I'm a showman." Well, can you imagine a world without Mickey Mouse?

**Presenter:** Peter Spencer, thank you.

### III. Listen and choose the best answer to each question you hear.

1. When was the film *Pinocchio* made?
2. How much did it cost to open Disneyland in Los Angeles in 1955?
3. How many Disneylands were mentioned by the two speakers?

## Part Four Here's More

### Exercise One

Hong Kong Disneyland is a theme park at Hong Kong Disneyland Resort. It was constructed by The Walt Disney Company and the Hong Kong Government on reclaimed land from the Penny's Bay, Lantau Island, Hong Kong, China. The park was officially opened to visitors at 13:00 local time on Monday, September 12, 2005; although VIPs and winners of a ticket lottery were allowed entry on a number of "test days" held before the grand opening. A unique feature of Hong Kong Disneyland is the widely use of two languages, English and Chinese (both in Traditional and Simplified forms) in its communication. On November 18, 2004, a special ceremony was held in the park to commemorate the placing of the tallest turret of Sleeping Beauty Castle. Present were Tung Chee Hwa, former Chief Executive of Hong Kong SAR; Jay Rasulo, president of Disney Parks and Resorts; Michael Eisner, CEO of the Walt Disney Company; and Mickey Mouse and other costumed characters. Hong Kong Disneyland has the shortest construction period among all Disneylands, possibly because it is the smallest Disneyland.

The park features four themed lands similar to those at other Disney Parks: Main Street, USA; Adventureland; Fantasyland; and Tomorrowland. It will also feature a daily parade and nightly fireworks.

### Exercise Two

During a 43-year Hollywood career that spanned the development of the motion picture medium as a modern American art, Walter Elias Disney, a modern Aesop, established himself and his product as a genuine part of American art. David Low, the late British political cartoonist, called Disney "the most significant figure in graphic arts since Leonardo."

A pioneer and innovator and the possessor of one of the most fertile imaginations the world has ever known, Walt Disney, along with members of his staff, received more than 950 honors and citations from every nation in the world, including 48 Academy Awards and seven Emmys in his lifetime. Walt Disney's personal awards included honorary degrees from Harvard, Yale, the University of Southern California, and UCLA; the Presidential Medal of Freedom; France's Legion of Honor and Officer d'Academie decorations; Thailand's Order of the Crown; Brazil's Order of the Southern Cross; Mexico's Order of the Aztec Eagle; and the Showman of the World Award from the National Association of Theatre Owners.

The creator of Mickey Mouse and founder of the Disneyland and Walt Disney World Theme Parks was born in Chicago, Illinois, on December 5, 1901. His father, Elias Disney, was Irish-Canadian. His mother, Flora Call Disney, was of German-American descent. Walt was one of five children, four boys and a girl.

# Unit 17 Global Warming

## Part Two Listen Now

### Text One

**Interviewer:** Dr. Clarke, global warming was the threat of the 1980s but it seems to have fizzled out of people's minds — why do you think that is?

**Dr. Clarke:** Yes, in a way you're right. I think scientists have become occupied with the task of trying to find out whether it really is happening and, if so, whether it's caused by human activity.

**Interviewer:** A greenhouse effect is, after all, a natural phenomenon …

**Dr. Clarke:** Yes, as we know, naturally occurring gases float above us, acting as insulators that prevent heat being radiated into space.

**Interviewer:** And the fear is that the insulation might get thicker …

**Dr. Clarke:** Yes, and because of this, the earth might get warmer.

**Interviewer:** The latest prediction we've heard is that temperature will increase by about a third of a degree every ten years. What are your feelings?

**Dr. Clarke:** Well … this prediction is difficult to make. You see the global climate is the result of a web of influences. Who is to say that a simple action such as adding carbon dioxide to the atmosphere will not have several effects which might even cancel each other out?

**Interviewer:** And I understand that the prediction is hard to verify whatever …

**Dr. Clarke:** Precisely.

**Interviewer:** Why is that?

**Dr. Clarke:** Because the earth's temperature surges and subsides naturally. In fact the best way of detecting global temperature change is to measure the temperature of the oceans as accurately as possible.

**Interviewer:** And this avoids the sort of seasonal fluctuations of the temperature of land mass.

**Dr. Clarke:** Yes — in fact an understanding of the oceans is crucial to understanding how the global climate works. The ocean transports heat around the globe. It's like a great reservoir of heat — a tiny change in sea surface temperature denotes a huge change in the amount of heat it is storing.

**IV. Listen to some parts of the interview and answer the following questions by choosing the right answer from the two choices marked *a* and *b*.**

1. **Interviewer:** Dr. Clarke, global warming was the threat of the 1980s but it seems to have fizzled out of people's minds — why do you think that is?

2. **Dr. Clarke:** I think scientists have become occupied with the task of trying to find out whether it really is happening and, if so, whether it's caused by human activity.

3. **Interviewer:** And the fear is that the insulation might get thicker …

   **Dr. Clarke:** Yes, and because of this, the earth might get warmer.

4. **Interviewer:** And I understand that the prediction is hard to verify whatever …

   **Dr. Clarke:** Precisely.

   **Interviewer:** Why is that?

5. **Dr. Clarke:** Because the earth's temperature surges and subsides naturally. In fact the best way of detecting global temperature change is to measure the temperature of the oceans as accurately as possible.

   **Interviewer:** And this avoids the sort of seasonal fluctuations of the temperature of land mass.

## Text Two

**Interviewer:** And now, I understand you are looking at ways of refining this measurement of ocean temperature.

**Dr. Clarke:** Yes. For a long time, we've measured it by placing thermometers in buoys bobbing in the oceans and also when ships draw water through their engines.

**Interviewer:** It's also been done by satellite, hasn't it?

**Dr. Clarke:** Yes. But now data from a more promising system is being collected. This is the European along-track scanning radiometer or ATSR, a much simpler name. The ATSR orbits the earth above us.

**Interviewer:** And what stage are you at with this?

**Dr. Clarke:** Well it's been up there two and a half years now. It's an infra-red detector that senses the earth's temperature with great accuracy and this is what we need … we have to be able to separate out random changes in temperature.

**Interviewer:** I believe there are other advantages as well?

**Dr. Clarke:** There are several … Every few days it covers the entire earth. So it produces large quantities of data. It measures the temperature from two angles, which allows correction for any effects that the intervening atmosphere may be having on its readings. Its field of view has a width of 500 km and it measures the temperature to 0.3 degree centigrade.

**Interviewer:** And it should go on for years?

**Dr. Clarke:** Yes.

**Interviewer:** Thank you, Dr. Clarke, for talking to us today … and now over to …

**IV. Listen to some parts of the interview and complete answers to the following questions.**

1. **Interviewer:** And now, I understand you are looking at ways of refining this measurement of ocean temperature.

   **Dr. Clarke:** Yes. For a long time, we've measured it by placing thermometers in buoys bobbing in the oceans and also when ships draw water through their engines.

2. **Dr. Clarke:** Yes. But now data from a more promising system is being collected. This is the European along-track scanning radiometer or ATSR, a much simpler name. The ATSR orbits the earth above us.

   **Interviewer:** And what stage are you at with this?

3. **Dr. Clarke:** Well it's been up there two and a half years now. It's an infra-red detector that senses the earth's temperature with great accuracy and this is what we need … we have to be able to separate out random changes in temperature.

4. **Dr. Clarke:** There are several … Every few days it covers the entire earth. So it produces large quantities of data. It measures the temperature from two angles, which allows correction for any effects that the intervening atmosphere may be having on its readings. Its field of view has a width of 500 km and it measures the temperature to 0.3 degree centigrade.

## Part Four Here's More

### Exercise One

All babies cry. It's normal, and it's a baby's number one way of saying anything. But it can make mothers very stressed! Research shows that the best thing to do with crying babies is always to comfort them quickly. It is not "spoiling" a baby and it will not make a baby weak. A baby who is not left to cry alone knows it is wanted and this will help the baby to be confident as it grows up. Usually a healthy baby will stop crying if it is given what it asks for. Research suggests that a baby who is regularly left crying may grow up with emotional problems.

### Exercise Two

A: What kind of differences have you noticed between teaching in the United States and in Chinese Hong Kong?

B: There are many common points, but there are some important differences. The main difference is that, when I am teaching English in the US, I am teaching what's called "English as a second language" — "ESL." This means that the students are living in an environment where English is spoken. In Chinese Hong Kong, we're working in what's largely referred to as an "English as a foreign language" — "EFL" environment. This means that English is not predominately the medium of communication.

## Exercise Three

**Driver:** Where to?

**Passenger:** Well, I'm going to the National Museum of Art, and ...

**Driver:** Sure. No problem.

**Passenger:** Uh, excuse me, how long does it take to get there?

**Driver:** Well, that all depends on the traffic, but it shouldn't take more than twenty minutes for the average driver.

**Passenger:** Okay. Uh, sorry for asking ...

**Driver:** Yeah?

**Passenger:** ... but do you have any idea how much the fare will be?

**Driver:** Oh, it shouldn't be more than 18 dollars ...

**Passenger:** Oh, and by the way, do you know what time the museum closes?

**Driver:** Well, I would guess around 6:00 o'clock.

**Passenger:** Uh, do you have the time?

**Driver:** Yeah. It's half past four.

**Passenger:** Thanks.

**Driver:** Uh, this IS your first time to the city, right?

**Passenger:** Yeah. How did you know?

**Driver:** Well, you can tell tourists from a mile away in this city because they walk down the street looking straight up at the skyscrapers.

**Passenger:** Was it that obvious?

**Driver:** Well ...

## Exercise Four

**Girl:** Dad, can I go to a movie with Sharon?

**Dad:** Yeah, sure. But wait, weren't you supposed to get a report card sometime this past week?

**Girl:** Well ... oh yeah ... Can I call Sharon now?

**Dad:** Uh-hum. You didn't answer my question. Did you receive it or not?

**Girl:** I love you Dad! You're the best!

**Dad:** Don't try to butter me up. I can guess that your answer means that you didn't do well in some of your classes.

**Girl:** Well, my English teacher is so boring, and he blows up every time someone talks.

**Dad:** In other words, you're not doing so well?

**Girl:** Uh, a C ... minus.

**Dad:** Oh. Well, how are you doing in your Spanish class? You said you liked that one.

**Girl:** Well, I do, but I forgot to turn in a couple of assignments, and I had problems on the last test. All those verbs tripped me up. I got them all mixed up in my head!

**Dad:** Okay, and what about algebra?

**Girl:** Ah, I'm acing that class. No sweat.

**Dad:** Oh!

**Girl:** Can I go now?

# Unit 18

# China in Professor Evans's Eyes

## Part Two Listen Now

### Text One

**Interviewer:** Professor Evans, I understand that you've lived in China for some three and a half years. Why did you choose to come to China?

**Prof. Evans:** Ever since I took some courses in college about Chinese history and Chinese language, I've been interested in China. So when I retired I decided to come to China, learn some Chinese language and learn something about Chinese culture and history. And at the same time, my teaching English here is a way of making a contribution to education in China.

**Interviewer:** What was your first impression of China?

**Prof. Evans:** I arrived at the Beijing airport. It was like any large international airport, very modern, nothing particularly exceptional. But then on the way to downtown Beijing I was immediately struck by the vast number of people to be seen everywhere: China is very densely populated. Lots of traffic, lots of people. The second major impression was the huge scale of things, the Forbidden City, Tian An Men Square, the Great Wall. Many public works in China are built to a very large scale. I found that fascinating.

**Interviewer:** Now you've been here for quite a few years. Do you notice any differences with the passage of time?

**Prof. Evans:** I have been here for three and a half years. In that time, Shanghai, where I've spent most of my time, has seen a great increase in the number of private cars. It seemed to me that the taxis used to outnumber private cars by far; now it is the other way around. There are about 45,000 taxis in Shanghai, but recently private cars are being added at the rate of 5,000 per month.

**Interviewer:** In some months, even more than that number, I think.

**Prof. Evans:** Possibly. The traffic is getting slower, because more and more cars are on the road with more and more traffic jams. More highways are being built, more roads widened, but not fast enough to keep up with the number of cars. If it keeps going this way long enough, the streets of Shanghai are destined to turn into permanent parking lots.

**Interviewer:** So you are worried about the situation.

**Prof. Evans:** Exactly. The number of bicycles seems to be getting smaller, and the city is making it harder for bicyclists by closing off many streets to bicyclists and getting rid of many bike lanes. For the city to discourage bicycles is a real shame, because of the health benefits to citizens, the lack of pollution and the speed, convenience and low cost of biking. They should instead be greatly encouraging bicycling as a major transportation mode.

And air pollution seems to be, if anything, worse than before, but I am not sure about that. On the other hand, people's attitudes tend to be more relaxed, more open to new ideas. And from conversations with people, I just notice that they are more and more willing to speak their mind. That is a very good sign that the society is becoming more open.

**III. Listen and choose the best answer to each question you hear.**

1. Why does Professor Evans decide to come to China?
2. What impressed Professor Evans most when he first came to China?
3. What is Professor Evans happy to see in Shanghai?

## Text Two

**Interviewer:** Adjustment to a new culture tends to occur in stages. At first it is very exciting, then it quickly becomes much more difficult. But after a certain amount of time passes, a person gets used to it and accepts the new culture. Do you think you have adapted to Chinese culture to some extent?

**Prof. Evans:** Yes, I do. Actually I didn't suffer from a large cultural shock, because I did a lot of preparation before I came. But some things you just cannot prepare for. I think the greatest cultural shock was just suddenly being surrounded by lots and lots of people and being in a place where the environmental quality is not very high. There is lots of pollution, air, water and noise. So those are the things that were hardest for me to get used to. The food, the customs and the people are wonderful. I have no problem at all with them. I've become a big fan of Chinese food and Chinese culture and really enjoy getting to know Chinese people.

**Interviewer:** Speaking of cultural shock, not all Chinese people are aware of cultural differences. So would you please give some advice to those people on how to get along with Americans?

**Prof. Evans:** Well, I think one of the main aspects about Americans is that almost all Americans are different from other Americans. So you cannot know one American and then assume that you can automatically understand other Americans. They come from many varied backgrounds culturally and ethnically. So that's something to keep in mind. Another thing, as many people have noted, Americans tend to be much more individualistic than Chinese. They greatly value privacy and their free time. That's something that is a bit different from the Chinese that I know, who often feel that if they are not with other people then they are not happy. Americans sometimes are very happy just to be quietly by themselves or to be with just a few others.

**Interviewer:** There are many Chinese people in the United States. Have you met some of them? Is there any difference between the Chinese abroad and the Chinese at home?

**Prof. Evans:** I've met many Chinese. There are all kinds of Chinese in the USA. Basically I don't find any difference between them and the Chinese in this country, other than that perhaps they tend to be more adventuresome or flexible, whether out of necessity or predilection. I suppose that they almost have to be, in order to leave the security of their home country, their family and friends, and to take a chance on living abroad. By the way, many of them arrive thinking America is some sort of paradise, some sort of heaven. But then they quickly find out that, no, it is not. That is, the immigrants end up working very, very hard, often harder, much harder, than they did in China. And they find that Americans also work extremely hard. Some Chinese in the United States often dream about returning to China where they would not have to work so hard and where they could be together with family and friends.

## Part Four Here's More

### Exercise

1. W: I heard you liked the play last night. I suppose your wife felt the same way about it.
   M: As a matter of fact, she left during the play.
   Q: What did we know about the man and his wife?
2. M: I can hardly believe that city has a population of 800,000.
   W: To be more exact, there are 813,400 there.
   Q: What is the population of that city?
3. M: May I borrow your hand calculator?
   W: Yes, but be sure to turn it off between problems so the battery won't wear out.
   Q: What shouldn't the man do?
4. W: Shanghai is beautiful and the weather is marvelous.
   M: Yes, and we can do some shopping here after we get checked in at the hotel.
   Q: What can we learn from the conversation?
5. W: Where are you going to visit this summer?
   M: I'm going to America for three weeks first and then I'll also visit London. I'll go to Australia last.
   Q: Which country is the man's second stop?
6. M: Didn't you advise Tommy against smoking?
   W: Yes, but whatever I say to him goes in one ear and out the other.
   Q: What does the woman mean?
7. M: Ah, you must be Kelly. Thanks for coming. It's hard to find a good baby sitter on a Friday night.
   W: Hi, Mr. Adams. I'd like to talk to you about my new rate increases. I've consulted with my mother, and she says I should charge more per child since I do the cooking and clean your house while you're away.
   Q: Why should the woman charge more for baby-sitting?
8. W: What are you doing this summer, John?
   M: Haven't decided yet, but there is a chance that I'll enroll in the summer session to try to finish my course requirements.
   Q: What is Adam most likely to do this summer?
9. W: I'm trying to buy a special birthday present for Linda. What about you?
   M: I lost my shirt while playing poker last night. I mean I can't afford anything now.
   Q: What does the man mean?
10. M: So, you'd like to share an apartment with one or two roommates within walking distance to school. And what's your budget like? I mean how much do you want to spend on rent?
    W: Uh, somewhere under 200 dollars a month, including utilities. Oh, and I'd love to rent a furnished apartment.
    Q: What kind of place is the woman looking for?

# Unit 19

## Spring Festival and Christmas

**Part Two Listen Now**

### Text One

**Interviewer:** The most important festival in the West is Christmas. Professor Evans, how do you celebrate it in China?

**Prof. Evans:** Christmas is the celebration of the birth of Christ. As a Christian, I would like to celebrate it with my family. Ideally, we would go to church and we have a big dinner, as well as open presents. On Christmas Eve, we have a quiet time. We'll read Bible verses about the birth of Christ. And we sing hymns, holy songs. Then we open up presents because presents symbolize the gift of Christ that God gave to humanity. The next morning, on Christmas Day, children discover that the stockings that were set out the night before have been filled by Santa Claus during the night. The stockings contain lots of small toys, candy and fruit. During Christmas we'll enjoy several nice meals together. And we'll just relax and take it easy and enjoy each other's company.

**Interviewer:** What is the most memorial gift you have received?

**Prof. Evans:** Since I have been in China, the most memorial gift that I have received is just having relatives to come over to visit. They themselves are a great gift because in China there is no time off for Christmas so I certainly have no time to fly back to the United States. The only way I can have Christmas with my family is for them to come here. They are without a doubt the most wonderful gift that I have received.

**Interviewer:** Christmas is not a Chinese festival, but in recent years we can feel the Christmas atmosphere in China, too. Many department stores and shops are decorated with Christmas trees and some people wear Santa hats for the season. Many young people send Christmas cards to their friends. What do you think of this phenomenon?

**Prof. Evans:** I think that many Chinese see Christmas celebrated in the West and then suppose that they can catch the Christmas spirit just by having Christmas trees, Santa Claus and an exchange of cards and gifts. But that's only part of what Christmas is about, and the least important part of that. I think it is impossible for a non-Christian to fully appreciate Christmas and to understand the true spirit of Christmas. There are, in fact, more and more Christians in China. But I think that on the whole the commercialization of Christmas in China, just like the commercialization of Christmas in the United States and other countries, really misses the point of Christmas. Commercial aspects are not very satisfying, and frequently take away from the real meaning of Christmas.

### Text Two

**Interviewer:** The most important festival in China is the Spring Festival. Have you celebrated it in China?

**Prof. Evans:** Yes, I have. I have been very fortunate to have been invited by dear Chinese friends into their homes and to have celebrated the Spring Festival with them. These have been some of the highlights of my stay in China.

**Interviewer:** Both Christmas and the Spring Festival are important holidays. Do they share something in common?

**Prof. Evans:** I think what they share in common is a coming together of the family, a reunion and an emphasis on large meals eaten together. On a superficial level, in the Spring Festival, just as with Christmas, there is also a strong gift-giving tradition, with the red envelops of money that are commonly given to children. So they have some things in common. But as far as the deeper spiritual meanings of the two festivals go, I don't think there is any relationship at all between them.

**Interviewer:** What do you think of the difference between the two festivals?

**Prof. Evans:** As I said, both are times of family reunion. There are the shared aspects of the giving of gifts, the emphasis on food, on spending time together with family. But differences are quite large. For example, for most Americans, most Christians, Christmas is a time of quiet reflection, prayer and thanksgiving. But for most Chinese, the Spring Festival is a very noisy time. It's a time of lots and lots of firecrackers and skyrockets. It is also a time of renewal for Chinese. They get new haircuts; buy new clothes; clean their houses, sweeping out the old year's bad luck and inviting in the new year's good luck; pay off debts; and basically get ready for a fresh start of a whole new year. But, certainly for most Chinese, it lacks any deep religious significance.

**Interviewer:** What attracts you most about the Spring Festival?

**Prof. Evans:** I am most fascinated by the great sacrifices that many Chinese make to be with their families during the Spring Festival. They travel vast distances, spending a lot of time, money and effort, to be with their families. And then there are many people who can not be with their families because they work in the transportation industry or other industries that everyone else relies on during the festival. So I really respect the sacrifice that these people make for the good of others because I know how much they, too, would like to be together with their families during the Spring Festival.

**Interviewer:** When celebrating the Spring Festival, does anything make you feel ill at ease?

**Prof. Evans:** Actually nothing makes me feel ill at ease. It did take some time to get used to the constant sound of loud firecrackers and "explosions" at all times of the day and night. The other thing that struck me was just how food is emphasized. Much has been written and said about traditional Spring Festival foods such as New Year's cake, meat-filled dumplings, and the round, sweet glutinous rice dumplings. Many of the food customs are regionally based, with North China's customs differing greatly from South China's, for instance.

But in my experience, what struck me most was the eating of pork during the Spring Festival. The Chinese family that I stayed with ate virtually every part of the pig. And at virtually every meal that we ate during the festival, there were lots and lots of various pork dishes and soups. It shows the importance of the pig in Chinese food culture. In fact, I think that pork is a kind of "comfort food" for many Chinese.

**Interviewer:** Especially for Southerners, I think.

**Prof. Evans:** Another aspect that is worth noting is that Chinese homes are frequently not heated very warmly by American standards. The first time when I was with a Chinese family for the Spring Festival, I was quite cold. Then I learned to dress more warmly, with layers upon layers of clothes. After that, there have been no problems. But in conclusion, I never felt ill at ease at all during the Spring Festival.

## Part Four Here's More

### Exercise One

In the 1600s, the first English immigrants left their own countries for New England for religious reasons. They wanted to live in a place where they could be free to have their own beliefs and there would be no official religion. So when this new country gained its independence in 1776, the separation of church and state was one of the basic laws for the United States. Attracted by the freedom of this land, more and more new immigrants have come to it and brought their own beliefs as well. Therefore, it is not surprising to easily find examples of every type of religion in the US. But most people fall into one of the two categories — Christian and Jewish.

The majority of Americans are Christians. They believe in Christ or Jesus. They celebrate Christmas — the birth of Christ, and Easter — the death and rebirth of Jesus. They think of Sunday as a holy day and worship in churches on that day. Just like Christians, Jews also believe in the existence of one God. But they don't believe that God has come to earth in any form. Every week Jewish people celebrate Holy Day from Friday evening to Saturday evening.

Since the second half of the twentieth century, there has been a decline in the strength of traditional religion in the United States. Recently, fewer people attend services regularly or think about traditional religious beliefs. However, religion still provides the customs and ceremonies which mark the most important events in a person's life, including birth, coming of age, marriage and death. Now churches are not only places for prayers and ceremonies; they are also community centers for educational, cultural and social activities.

### Exercise Two

The predominate religion in America today is Christianity. This has been historically true from the founding of America until the present. Christian beliefs have been a major influence in the forming of America. The Bible has been the guiding book of most of its leaders and its documents. However, like in most countries in the world, America also has had leaders who use religion for their own political ends while not living according to its teachings.

# Unit 20

# Teaching English to Chinese University Students

## Part Two Listen Now

### Text One

**Interviewer:** Professor Evans, how long have you been teaching English at East China Normal University?

**Prof. Evans:** Well, for three and a half years, since I first came to China.

**Interviewer:** What do you think of your students' English level?

**Prof. Evans:** I teach several hundred students advanced reading and also have a number of conversation classes. I am impressed by their basic grasp of grammar and basic understanding of Western culture. They also tend to be quick to learn new vocabulary. On the other hand, I find that they don't have many opportunities to speak or listen to English. Consequently, speaking and listening tend to be their weak points.

**Interviewer:** When you teach English, which do you attach greater importance to, cultural knowledge or language itself?

**Prof. Evans:** Actually I think culture and language are inseparable. They really shouldn't, indeed cannot be, separated. But in language classes, I do emphasize the spoken or the written language. By the time they arrive at the university the students are well trained in grammar and many of the technological points of English. So I don't emphasize that as much as how to use language in daily situations.

**Interviewer:** What do you think your students are more interested in, cultural knowledge or the language itself?

**Prof. Evans:** Some are more interested in language. Some are more interested in culture. The students also see them as inseparable. The students want to experience American culture through me, since I am a native English speaker with a lifetime of experience in the US. Often in my language classes what I talk about includes a lot of culture and cultural background of the language.

**Interviewer:** Have you found any language problems that are common among Chinese learners of English? Can you give some advice to them?

**Prof. Evans:** First I should say again that one of the nice things is that most Chinese students have a good grasp of English grammar. Furthermore, their pronunciation is usually not too bad at all. Their biggest problem is their hesitancy to speak out, to open their mouths, talk and exchange ideas. This is as much a cultural problem as a linguistic one. Perhaps I shouldn't say it's a "problem"; I should say it's a "phenomenon." My advice to them is to relax. Don't be afraid to make mistakes. When they do make the inevitable mistakes they should not worry about what other people may think. They should just try to communicate as much as possible, at every opportunity. That way they will be more open and I think they'll become better, more fluent communicators in English.

### III. Listen and choose the best answer to each question you hear.

1. Which is NOT mentioned when Professor Evans talks about Chinese students' English level?
2. Which statement is true about the relationship between cultural knowledge and language itself?
3. Which is NOT suggested by Professor Evans?

## Text Two

**Interviewer:** Professor Evans, what do you think of students' participation in class? It is said Chinese students are less active than American students in class. Is that true?

**Prof. Evans:** In general I think it is true. There are several reasons for this. One reason is that Chinese classes are very large by American standards, so students have to be a bit subdued, otherwise the classroom might get too noisy. But the fundamental reason is not the high numbers of students, but rather that the Chinese students are trained from a young age to know their place, to respect authority and not to speak out if they aren't called upon specifically. In fact, the basic way that Chinese learn is by observation, not by experimentation.

**Interviewer:** In a way, it is the case.

**Prof. Evans:** So in consequence, the students in class are writing down lots of notes, sometimes seeming to write down every word that the professor says. Their place is not to question, but rather, as it were, to be empty vessels into which their teachers pour knowledge. They carry on a long tradition of Chinese education by observation and passive acceptance, not education by participation, challenge or experimentation. It is a tradition that goes back several thousand years.

**Interviewer:** I hear in America, students are encouraged to think and speak out their ideas, no matter what these ideas may be. Is that right?

**Prof. Evans:** I think, broadly speaking, that is correct. There are limits, of course. It depends on the teacher, for one thing. But in general students are encouraged to be creative and actively share their ideas with other people on the theory that one creative idea may beget another creative idea, that one student's idea may stimulate another's. Of course, on the one hand this can tend to be somewhat time-consuming or even wasteful, if there is little or nothing that comes of it. But on the other hand, as an exercise, it encourages students to think deeply and to try to be as creative as they can be. It is a kind of learning by doing or by questioning oneself or others.

**Interviewer:** To what extent have you found that Chinese students can express their own ideas instead of just absorbing their teachers' ideas?

**Prof. Evans:** I find that when Chinese students speak up, they usually express their own ideas rather well. But the tendency is for them not to speak up. When they don't speak, how do you know what they are thinking? Maybe they have their own ideas. Maybe they are just passively absorbing the teachers' ideas. You just don't know. Of course, I think all Chinese students, like pupils everywhere, are individuals and in general they do have their own ideas. But many of them are very hesitant to share their ideas with other people. Sometimes it seems as if they feel it is not their place to stand out or rock the boat by challenging orthodoxy (that is, the knowledge that is handed down from their teachers) or even to publicly hold an opinion.

**Interviewer:** In China, students seldom drop out of school in order to make money and then return to school again to continue their education. What about American students?

**Prof. Evans:** American students sometimes do this. As we all know, education is expensive. So schools in America tend to be very helpful and flexible for students who are in financial need. They also understand that students sometimes need time off to grow, to mature, away from school. So this flexibility is, I think, one of the strong points of American education. In China, it is much more difficult for students to change directions. This is true whether it is something that should be simple, such as changing their majors, or whether it is something more complicated, such as dropping out of school and then dropping back in again. But there are great changes taking place in education in China. I have noticed more and more of my students have started to get part-time jobs either as tutors or even in various companies during their spring break and during the summer. But by and large, most Chinese students still haven't had a job by the time they graduate. Their parents' expectation is that while their children are students they should spend their time studying, not working at a part-time job.

**Interviewer:** This attitude is gradually changing, I believe. OK, thank you for spending time answering my questions.

### III. Listen and choose the best answer to each question you hear.

1. What is the main reason why Chinese students are usually passive in class?
2. According to this interview, which is NOT the difference between American students and Chinese students?
3. Which of the statements is NOT true about Chinese students?

## Part Four Here's More

### Exercise

1. Mathew shows a lot of enthusiasm for the tennis course, and I wish he would show as much for studies.
2. It's a real scorching day today, and the forecasters are saying that there is no end in sight.
3. It sounds really good to have dinner with you. But I have to finish my history paper today and hand it in tomorrow.
4. Do you ever hear Miss Smith sing a song? Yesterday she just produced a series of sounds that corresponded closely with the score of "Home, Sweet Home."
5. You said you don't want to live in the dormitory next year. You need some privacy. But check out the cost of renting an apartment first and I wouldn't be surprised if you change your mind.
6. I hear Mitchell turned down that job. Well, the hours were convenient, but she won't be able to make ends meet.
7. You say you really like those abstract paintings we saw in our art history class today, but I guess it's something I haven't acquired a taste for yet.
8. Your parents are coming to see your apartment this weekend? Looks as if I'd better lend you my vacuum cleaner then.
9. You say that George is going to work in New York for the summer, but can he do that and also go to summer school?
10. You seem to be quite optimistic about what this country is faced with. As far as you've explained the financial situation, it doesn't sound too bad.

# Appendix II
# Answer Key

## Unit 1
## Clothes

### Part One Before You Listen

*II.* Text One d Text Two a, b, c

### Part Two Listen Now

**Text One**

*III.* 1. d 2. b 3. a

*IV.* 1. special dresses 2. wedding 3. tuxedoes
4. parties 5. special and fancy dresses 6. sports events
7. family get-togethers 8. slacks 9. jeans
10. knit skirts 11. cotton shirts 12. cotton blouses
13. sweaters

**Text Two**

*III.* 1. The working environment. 2. It's more economical and creative.
3. Red, beige, navy and grey.

*IV.* 1. social status 2. shirts and casual pants, suit
3. more clothes 4. feel good, particular fashion trends

### Part Four Here's More

**Exercise**

1. Most people buy their clothes. But I enjoy making some of my clothes.
2. For a long time, black seemed to be a popular, important color. Everyone needed to have a black dress for some occasions.

3. The fashion show is three blocks away. Walk till you go to the traffic lights and turn right. It is right there.
4. We usually sit together and talk first and then maybe serve something to drink.
5. All of these seem like very individualistic reasons for divorcing.
6. Bus travel tends to be the cheapest form of transportation.
7. But then perhaps they tend to be more adventuresome.
8. So in my language classes I often include a lot of cultural knowledge.
9. Perhaps I shouldn't say it's a problem, I should say it's a phenomenon.
10. Many people are not able to be with their families.
11. Of course, this can also tend to be somewhat time-wasting if there are not any important ideas that are brought up.
12. They look for those kinds of similarities.
13. And it seems in America there's just something for everyone of all different economic groups.
14. So in wintertime, when they retire, people like to go down south in warmer climate.
15. And they must have some pride and be involved in the profession and share their profession with others.

# Unit 2 Food

## Part One Before You Listen

***II.*** Text One a Text Two b

## Part Two Listen Now

**Text One**

***III.*** 1. Pumpkin pie.

2. a. shortening b. blender; shortening c. Push d. plate
e. eggs; spices f. top; pan g. Bake; an hour; temperature

3. Her husband. 4. A variety of types. 5. A couple of hours.

***IV.*** 1. T 2. F 3. F 4. T 5. F

**Text Two**

***III.*** 1. cereal, milk, fruit, toast wit jam, coffee, juice, scrambled eggs, fried eggs, pancakes

2. sandwiches, soups 3. vegetables, meat 4. soup or salad

5. casserole, stir-fry dish, roast, vegetables, fruit, salad 6. dessert, coffee

***IV.*** 1. Dinner. 2. Having a picnic, eating outdoor, cooking chicken on the grill.

3. Around the table. 4. On the left side of the plate on top of the napkin.
5. Sharp side in on the right side of the plate.
6. Next to the knife. 7. Above the knife at the top of the plate.

## Part Four Here's More

**Exercise One**

Passage One c, b, a Passage Two b, a, d, c, e

**Exercise Two**

Passage One

a. Heat; salt; boiling b. mix c. Add; mixture
d. Stir; thick e. add f. Stir; thick
g. Cool; store

Passage Two

a. Scrape; table b. cover; paper; iron c. Remove; repeat; lifted

# Unit 3 Real Estate

## Part One Before You Listen

*II.* Text One a, b Text Two a, c, d

## Part Two Listen Now

**Text One**

*III.* 1. T 2. F 3. F 4. F 5. T 6. T

*IV.* 1. The interest rates for mortgage were high.
2. 15 hours.
3. When he/she is trying to find houses for some buyers.
4. Market value and previous sales of the same type of houses.
5. Rent some space to store the stuff.

**Text Two**

*III.* 1. a 2. b 3. c 4. b 5. d

*IV.* 1. there are different types of property
2. 1,848; 140,000; the market is tight
3. 121,000; 271,737
4. the most expensive; 313,300; its average market time

5. 100,000; 12,000; keep the park and the services

6. mortgage limit/purchase price limit; mortgage interest rate; private mortgage insurance

## Part Four Here's More

### Exercise One

1. 317; 17A  2. 3.18  3. 60.6  4. 2:50

5. 30% / 30 percent  6. 418,600  7. 70,000  8. 1,432,266,043

### Exercise Two

1. M9301274  2. 17  3. 025796363  4. (02)5791857

5. 8639993  6. SO23 9DY  7. 31, 1968  8. 01316883155

9. 772508  10. 60877422

# Unit 4 Transportation and Traveling

## Part One Before You Listen

***II.*** Text One a  Text Two c

## Part Two Listen Now

### Text One

***III.*** 1. car, bicycle, foot  2. parking, expensive  3. commuter train

4. newspaper, a cup of coffee, day's work, mobile phone, to people

5. medium sized  6. 45  7. 8:30

***IV.*** 1. T  2. T  3. F (It costs much less than that.)  4. T  5. F (They go to work by car.)

### Text Two

***III.*** 1. d  2. c  3. a  4. c  5. a

***IV.*** 1. college  2. summer; three  3. late 1960s

4. comfortable  5. special promotions; special inexpensive tickets

## Part Four Here's More

### Exercise

***I.*** 1. B  2. C  3. A

***II.*** 1. Commuter trains and subway trains.

2. By car.

3. By different colors and numbers.
4. Pay a fee or a percent of the original fare.
5. No. Prices vary.
6. Book the ticket early.
7. In carpools, several people travel together to work in one car and share the cost.
8. People involved can use special lanes that enable them to move more quickly during rush hours.

# Unit 5

# Transportation and Traveling (Continued)

## Part One Before You Listen

*II.* Text One b Text Two a

## Part Two Listen Now

### Text One

*III.* 1. To travel by plane in China is quite expensive for a Chinese income.
2. Book the ticket two months in advance or even earlier.
3. New York.
4. They cost almost the same because the price of the ticket does not depend on the distance traveled but on the number of people traveling a particular route. From Minneapolis to Rapid City, there's only one major airline and no competition at all. The monopoly allows them to keep high the price of the ticket.

*IV.* 1. T 2. F 3. F

### Text Two

*III.* 1. during the week
2. over Labor Day, Independence Day, Easter or during a paid vacation
3. during the summer
4. at Christmas, Thanksgiving and Spring Break
5. during the summer
6. during the winter

*IV.* 1. a 2. c 3. d 4. a 5. a 6. b 7. c 8. d

## Part Four Here's More

### Exercise

1. since 1948; special celebrations; attitudes of Americans; focus to teach children
2. in February; 22nd; 12th; first president; Civil War; singled out; 1971; decided; discontinued; replaced; celebrate; birthdays; all US presidents
3. oldest; lost their lives; Declaration Day; takes place
4. dedicated; US workers; 1882; celebrated annually
5. discovery of a group; led to; colonization; native Americans; pleased about; bad sense; continent; had been living
6. in honor of; who died; buried; overlooking; focal point; Similar ceremonies; each nation's; France; November 11th; World War I; 1918; became known; received its name; 1926; national holiday; requested to make this day; recognizing that peace; signed the bill; national ceremonies; 11.00 a.m.; military services; laid

# Unit 6

# Marriage and Family

## Part One Before You Listen

***II.*** Text One c Text Two b

## Part Two Listen Now

### Text One

***III.*** 1. F 2. T 3. F 4. T 5. F

***IV.*** 1. No. Dating has changed to some extent.
2. He had a girl that would call him on the phone. And they would call every night and they would talk to each other on the phone. They didn't go anywhere and they didn't go out on a date.
3. He meant they were a couple.
4. It means you can drive a car and go out with your date in a car.
5. They should be attracted towards each other.
6. In school, in their recreational hobbies, in places where they have a like interest, in church, at a baseball field, or somewhere they can do something in general.

### Text Two

***III.*** 1. c 2. c 3. b 4. c 5. b 6. c

***IV.*** 1. local state 2. minister; church; religious
3. difficult 4. expensive

5. 26; 28
6. financial independence; resourcefulness
7. obedient

## Part Four Here's More

### Exercise One

1. F 2. T 3. F

### Exercise Two

1. marry; marriage
2. cookies and punch; sit-down; local hotel; dance; private
3. wedding gifts
4. religious; civil
5. marry
6. old; new; borrowed; blue
7. regarded; groom
8. the newly married couple

# Unit 7 Divorce

## Part One Before You Listen

*II.* Text One a Text Two c

## Part Two Listen Now

### Text One

*III.* 1. b 2. c 3. d 4. c

*IV.* 1. 20%; 25%; one; married women

2. not increasing

3. a. meet; emotional needs b. No-Fault; 1973

### Text Two

*III.* 1. 75%; affected

2. 3; 4

3. stigma; divorce; negative

4. greatly increased; peak; maintained about the same; decreased

*IV.* 1. F 2. T 3. F 4. T

## Part Four Here's More

### Exercise One

1. Teaching the first grade.

2. Losing temper.
3. Dealing with the stress of the job.
4. Best age.
5. Difference between the ways girls and boys perform.
6. Whether people hug in a Japanese family.
7. Difference in eye contact.
8. Courses at the college.
9. Advice to school leavers.
10. Immediate plans.

### Exercise Two

***I.*** 1. **Detailed:** needs and demands; safety
**Generalized:** passenger comfort
2. **Disadvantages of the career:** glamorous; very hard; one's family and social life
**Advantages of the career:** Rewarding and challenging; boring

***II.*** 1. I suppose, if I have to come up with a single answer, ...
2. but, all the same, ...

# Unit 8 Divorce (Continued)

## Part One Before You Listen

***II.*** Text One a, b Text Two d

## Part Two Listen Now

### Text One

***III.*** 1. a. People get scared by the high divorce rate and they do the opposite to try to maintain marriage as possible as they can.
b. It's possible that fewer people are getting married.
2. To reconsider how selfish you are being.
3. No, it's necessary in some cases.
4. a. Are you being honest with your spouse?
b. Do you trust your spouse?
c. Do you say things that are hurtful to your spouse?
d. Do you say things in front of your children or to your children that indicate you don't respect or trust your spouse?
5. a. The most intimate setting.

b. The most violent setting.

6. a. It's very easy to be critical of somebody else.

   b. It's very easy to be selfish and not give up things that you might really like.

***IV.*** 1. T 2. F 3. T 4. T

**Text Two**

***III.*** 1. 20 years old
2. 6 months after having met them
3. engaged for more than 3 years
4. your parents or your siblings
5. divorced
6. socio-economic background
7. before you're married; immediate plans to get married

***IV.*** 1. Because it might show kind of a lack of commitment, a lack of saying "Yes, OK, I will settle down now and get married to you."
2. It may show that you don't know how to deal with conflict or how to communicate effectively.
3. They might not even trust the institution of marriage and remain single throughout their life.
4. An extra set of challenges. There might be stereotypes or prejudices.

## Part Four Here's More

**Exercise**

1. a. Physical training or exercise program.
   b. Psychological program.
   c. Discussion groups.
2. a. Reading about, listening to or watching baseball.
   b. Get some sort of exercise every day.
   c. Work hard at keeping personal relationships at the peak.
3. a. Kids who are supported.
   b. Kids whose parents value education.
   c. Kids who have computers at home in their bedroom.
4. a. It produces large quantities of data.
   b. It measures the temperature from two angles.
   c. Its field of view has a width of 500 km and it measures temperature to 0.3 degree centigrade.

# Unit 9

# Teaching at High School and University

## Part One Before You Listen

***II.*** Text One b, c, d Text Two b, c

## Part Two  Listen Now

### Text One

***III.*** 1. c  2. a  3. b  4. d

***IV.*** 1. a bachelor's degree with a defined teaching major; the Teaching Education Program; experiences of teaching

2. has many years' actual teaching experience
3. earn hours of credits; a rise/an increase
4. is not very well paid; like working with people; concerned about making money

### Text Two

***III.*** 1. c  2. b  3. b  4. c

***IV.***

1. Enjoy the active teaching
2. Disciplining
3. the content area
4. the area they are majoring in
5. helping them
6. older young people
7. working at lessons
8. Like themselves
9. Feel good
10. have some pride
11. many other rewards
12. Motivate students to study/see the value in learning
13. education is important
14. learning styles
15. there is a science
16. How to make learning practical

## Part Four  Here's More

### Exercise

1. twelve
2. five
3. kindergarten
4. five
5. sixth
6. twelfth
7. awarded
8. undergraduate
9. associate
10. major
11. specialize
12. continue
13. exceptions
14. MBA
15. six
16. course
17. ability
18. thesis

# Unit 10 Campus Life

## Part One  Before You Listen

***II.*** Text One  a, b, d    Text Two  c, d

## Part Two Listen Now

### Text One

*III.* 1. Rachel
2. St. Olaf College
3. Studio Art and Education
4. Senior year
5. An Art class
6. An Art History class
7. A linguistic course
8. A Figure and Drawing class
9. talk to roommates
10. meet some friends
11. for a coffee
12. for sports
13. a waitress at a restaurant
14. a gas station
15. to pay for tuition cost and books
16. to pay for a car
17. insurance
18. to pay for a trip

*IV.* 1. F 2. T 3. T 4. F

### Text Two

*III.* 1. d 2. c 3. b

*IV.* 1. thinking about getting married
2. she's had a lot of fun with her friends and has learned a lot
3. she could make new friends and have a lot of fun
4. teach Art; an international school

## Part Four Here's More

### Exercise

1. Some are specialized in certain fields of study while some are general universities with degrees offered in many fields.
2. Entrance exams and SAT exams are usually required, and a minimum score on SAT is necessary for university entrance.
3. Students whose parents pay taxes in a given state and who themselves have lived in that state for at least a year before going to university.
4. Most students live in dormitories on campus.

# Unit 11 Anna in Australia

## Part One Before You Listen

*II.* Text One a, c     Text Two b, c, d

## Part Two Listen Now

### Text One

***III.*** 1. Two　　2. nutritional science　　3. the local council

***IV.*** 1. college

2. provides food for the older people in the community who can't get out of their flat or their house

3. outgoing

4. to change courses

### Text Two

***III.*** 1. The way Australians sometimes express themselves in everyday life.

2. The rate at which the body burns up food.

***IV.*** 1. a. interviews and talk-back programs on radio

b. the expressions that she hears

2. a. 20

c. didn't have any breakfast at all; ate foods for breakfast that were too high in sugar

3. a. the local council; more experience

b. hospital

c. own business; nutritional advice; consultation; her own country; the diet of her people at home

## Part Four Here's More

### Exercise One

1. Equipment or facilities.
2. It is a form that indicates that they are giving permission for the student to study in their program.
3. English as a second language.
4. In a special room called the reserve room.

### Exercise Two

1. b　　2. a　　3. b　　4. a

# Unit 12 Working on Board the Plane

## Part One Before You Listen

***II.*** Text One　b, c, d　　Text Two　b, d

## Part Two Listen Now

### Text One

***III.*** 1. c 2. d 3. a

***IV.*** 1. T 2. F 3. T 4. F

### Text Two

***III.*** 1. b 2. a 3. c

***IV.*** 1. regularly changing the time on her watch/regularly adjusting her watch

2. the smoking restrictions; the upgrading of the meals
3. more pleasant atmosphere; reduced fire risk
4. challenging; rewarding; very hard; glamorous

## Part Four Here's More

### Exercise One

1. c 2. c 3. d 4. d 5. b 6. c 7. d 8. a 9. d 10. c

### Exercise Two

1. Dentist
2. Good with the hands
3. Hard-working, bright, cheerful, creative
4. Secretary
5. Good, fast, accurate shorthand and typing, good at English and spelling
6. Loyal, reliable, sense of humor
7. Housewife
8. Able to cook, clean, nurse, decorate
9. Energetic, hard-working
10. Fireman
11. Good at working in a team, able to make quick decisions, know how to use equipment
12. Courageous, caring about people
13. Stewardess/air hostess/flight attendant
14. Able to speak a foreign language, able to work as a waitress and an interpreter
15. Friendly, good-looking, hard-working

# Unit 13 Achieving Career Success

## Part One Before You Listen

***II.*** Text One a, b Text Two a, c

## Part Two Listen Now

### Text One

***III.*** 1. b 2. d 3. c

***IV.*** 1. He should get a sales job in a retail establishment.

2. He reads inspirational books as well as listens to motivational tapes.
3. He was determined to accomplish what he set out to do.
4. He thought his job was to think and ask new questions.

### Text Two

***III.*** 1. F 2. T 3. F 4. F

***IV.*** 1. getting face to face with clients

2. he was doing the job for himself
3. a few personality traits
4. talk and find out what is best for the client; help them make a decision

## Part Four Here's More

### Exercise One

1. b 2. c 3. b 4. d 5. a 6. d 7. b 8. c 9. a 10. d

### Exercise Two

1. b 2. c 3. d 4. a 5. b 6. b 7. a 8. c 9. a 10. c

# Unit 14 Farming

## Part One Before You Listen

***II.*** Text One b, c Text Two b, c

## Part Two Listen Now

### Text One

***III.*** 1. a 2. c 3. d 4. c 5. b

***IV.*** 1. profitable; fluctuates; production costs; bring on; make an investment; insecure

2. conveniences; relaxation; enjoys; kill

### Text Two

***III.*** 1. a 2. c 3. b 4. d 5. d

***IV.*** 1. T 2. T 3. T 4. F 5. F

## Part Four Here's More

**Exercise**

1. insecurity; under contract
2. labor unions
3. series
4. not true
5. a difference
6. impersonal
7. what sort of problems
8. thousand-dollar coffin; six months

# Unit 15 People Skills

## Part One Before You Listen

***II.*** Text One c, d Text Two c, d

## Part Two Listen Now

**Text One**

***III.*** 1. c 2. b 3. c 4. a

***IV.*** 1. educated; socialized; need to succeed

2. surprised; lacked; firing; consultant

3. pause; announce; put down; due attention; approach; hold on

**Text Two**

***III.*** 1. a, b, c 2. a, c, d 3. a, b, d

***IV.*** 1. I'm sorry, I didn't get your name

2. extend

3. honest and pleasant; there were so many interesting people I met

4. blocked your name

## Part Four Here's More

**Exercise One**

1. She sat two rows in front of us. She had a bright yellow shirt on.
   sat two：/sæ-tuː/ 省音；rows in：/rəʊ-zɪn/ 连读；front of us：/frɔ-tə-fəs/ 连读和弱读；had a：/hæ-də/ 连读；bright yellow：/braɪ-tʃeləʊ/ 同化；shirt on：/ʃɛː-tɔn/ 连读
2. Would you mind my sitting here?
   Would you：/wʊ-dʒə/ 同化
3. And I want to see if his band can play at my birthday party.

And I：/ən-daɪ/ 弱读和连读；want to：/wɔn-tə/ 省音和弱读

4. I've had enough. I don't know what to think of her anymore.
   had enough：/hæ-dɪnʌf/ 连读；don't know：/dəʊn-nəʊ/ 省音；what to：/wɔ-tə/ 省音和弱读；think of：/θɪn-kəv/ 连读和弱读
5. Mary looks so different now.
   looks so：/lʊk-sə/ 省音；different now：/dɪfərən-naʊ/ 省音
6. I heard that you just quit. I just can't believe it.
   heard that you：/hɛː-ðɛ-tʃə/ 省音和同化；just quit：/dʒʌs-kwɪt/ 省音；just can't believe it：/dʒʌs-kæn-bɪliː-vɪt/ 省音和连读
7. The waiter repeated, "Cash or charge?" But the foreign visitor still couldn't understand him.
   But the：/bʌ-ðə/ 省音；couldn't：/kʊdn/ 省音
8. I'm throwing out the food that made you sick at dinner the other night.
   out the：/aʊ-ðə/ 省音；food that：/fuː-ðæ/ 省音；made you：/meɪ-dʒə/ 同化；sick at：/sɪ-kət/ 连读和弱读
9. I got you the book you wanted. Here it is.
   got you：/gɔ-tʃə/ 同化；book you：/bʊ-kjuː/ 连读；Here it is：/hɪə-rɪ-tɪz/ 连读
10. This test ranks your abilities.
    test ranks you：/tes-ræŋk-ʃə/ 省音和同化
11. She made those rolls you like. So why not come and have some?
    made those：/meɪ-ðəʊz/ 省音；rolls you：/rəʊl-ʒə/ 同化；not come：/nɔ-kʌm/ 省音；and：/ən/ 弱读
12. He's trying to get hold of you.
    to：/tə/ 弱读；get hold of you：/ge-təʊ-də-vjə/ 连读和弱读

**Exercise Two**

1. lunch order is here
2. She's in a
3. She's on
4. What about hot ham and cheese
5. four and a half
6. If it's OK
7. Life is old
8. like a breeze
9. Take me home
10. Painted on
11. Teardrop in
12. voice in
13. get a feeling
14. should have been home

# Unit 16

## Magic Disney World

### Part One　Before You Listen

***II.*** Text One　a, c, d　　Text Two　a, b, c

## Part Two Listen Now

### Text One

*III.* 1. creator 2. inventor 3. Walt Disney World
4. 1901 5. Chicago 6. American Red Cross
7. the First World War 8. Kansas City 9. experimental-type films
10. California 11. Roy 12. 1928
13. artists and illustrators

*IV.* 1. correspondence course 2. Oswald the Rabbit
3. talking cartoon film 4. business manager; imaginative, creative part of the partnership

### Text Two

*III.* 1. b 2. c 3. a

*IV.* 1. F 2. F 3. T 4. F

## Part Four Here's More

### Exercise One

1. theme park 2. Hong Kong government 3. September 12, 2005
4. unique feature 5. communication 6. November 18, 2004
7. Sleeping Beauty Castle 8. costumed characters 9. construction period
10. Adventureland 11. Tomorrowland 12. nightly fireworks

### Exercise Two

1. He thought that Disney was the most significant figure in graphic arts since Leonardo.
2. More than 950, including 48 Academy Awards and seven Emmys in his lifetime.
3. Four.
4. Seven.
5. His father was of Irish-Canadian descent and his mother was of German-American descent.

# Unit 17 Global Warming

## Part One Before You Listen

*II.* Text One c Text Two b

## Part Two  Listen Now

**Text One**

***III.*** 1. F  2. T  3. T  4. F  5. T  6. T

***IV.*** 1. b  2. b  3. b  4. a  5. a

**Text Two**

***III.*** 1. thermometers  2. satellite  3. ATSR
4. accuracy  5. data  6. correction; angles
7. 500 km  8. 0.3 degree

***IV.*** 1. ocean temperature  2. the use of ATSR  3. great accuracy
4. ATSR

## Part Four  Here's More

**Exercise One**

1. Babies' crying.  2. Comforting a crying baby quickly.

**Exercise Two**

1. English is spoken  2. medium of communication

**Exercise Three**

1. How long it'll take to get to the National Museum of Art.
2. Tourists.

**Exercise Four**

1. report card  2. verbs

# Unit 18

# China in Professor Evans's Eyes

## Part One  Before You Listen

***II.*** Text One  b, c, d  Text Two  b, c

## Part Two  Listen Now

**Text One**

***III.*** 1. a  2. d  3. c

***IV.*** 1. F  2. T  3. T  4. F  5. F  6. T

**Text Two**

***III.*** 1. There are lots of people around and the environmental quality is not very high.
2. Almost all Americans are different from other Americans. / Americans come from many

different cultural and ethnical backgrounds.

3. The Chinese in the US tend to be more adventuresome or flexible.

***IV.*** 1. do some preparation; Chinese food, customs, culture and people

2. privacy and their free time

3. not a paradise/heaven; work much harder; they would not have to work so hard and could be together with family and friends

## Part Four Here's More

**Exercise**

1. b 2. c 3. b 4. d 5. a 6. c 7. c 8. b 9. c 10. d

# Unit 19

# Spring Festival and Christmas

## Part One Before You Listen

***II.*** Text One a, b, c Text Two c, d

## Part Two Listen Now

**Text One**

***III.*** 1. d 2. c 3. b

***IV.*** 1. T 2. F 3. F 4. T 5. F 6. T

**Text Two**

***III.*** 1. a, b, c, i, k 2. a, b, c, e, f, h, j, l

***IV.*** 1. He feels the experiences are some of the highlights of his stay in China. / He feels the experiences are some of the most memorial ones of his stay in China.

2. On religious level.

3. Because they make great sacrifice for the good of others.

4. New Year's cake, meat-filled dumplings and round sweet glutinous rice dumplings.

5. Because the Chinese family he stayed with cooked various pork dishes and soups for virtually every meal during the Spring Festival.

6. No, he wasn't.

## Part Four Here's More

**Exercise One**

1. T 2. T 3. T 4. F 5. F 6. F 7. T

### Exercise Two

The predominate religion in America today is Christianity. This has been historically true from the founding of America until the present. Christian beliefs have been a major influence in the forming of America. The Bible has been the guiding book of most of its leaders and its documents. However, like in most countries in the world, America also has had leaders who use religion for their own political ends while not living according to its teachings.

# Unit 20

# Teaching English to Chinese University Students

## Part One Before You Listen

***II.*** Text One a, b, d Text Two c, d

## Part Two Listen Now

### Text One

***III.*** 1. b 2. c 3. d

***IV.*** 1. Advanced reading and conversation.

2. Spoken and written language used in daily situation.
3. Because he is a native English speaker with a lifetime of experience in the US.
4. The hesitancy to speak out.

### Text Two

***III.*** 1. b 2. d 3. d

***IV.*** 1. know their place; respect authority; question (teachers); passive acceptance; participation; challenge

2. one creative idea may beget another one/one student's idea may stimulate another's; there is little or nothing coming of it; think deeply
3. not to speak up; hold an opinion publicly
4. can't afford education/are in financial need; want to grow/mature

## Part Four Here's More

### Exercise

1. c 2. b 3. c 4. c 5. b 6. a 7. c 8. c 9. a 10. b